# THE
# SILENT WORK

## by
# KNOWLEDGE KING

# The Silent Work by Knowledge King



Knowledge King Publishing
PO Box 310501
Atlanta, GA 31131

ISBN: 9798218931391
LCCN: 2026902972

Ordering Information:
Quantity sales. Special discounts are available on quantity purchases by corporations, associations, and others. For details, contact the publisher at the address above.
Orders by U.S. trade bookstores and wholesalers. Please contact Distribution:
Tel: (404) 449-3186
Email: knowledgeking129@gmail.com

Printed in the United States of America

# Preface

There are books that are conceived in a single spark - arriving all at once like lightning in the night. The Silent Work was not one of them. It did not rush, nor demand to be written in a moment of urgency. Instead, it approached slowly, with the quiet patience of dawn breaking across the horizon. Its presence was felt long before its words ever reached the page.

At first, it was only a faint stirring - a subtle awareness that something within me was shifting. There was no voice, no grand revelation, no sudden command to write. There was simply an inner pull toward Silence, toward a different way of knowing, toward a truth that could not be spoken loudly because it is not heard in noise. It revealed itself gradually, step by step, as I learned to sit with myself more honestly, to listen without seeking answers, and to honor the spaces between thoughts.

The ideas that eventually became this book were not delivered in a single vision, but gathered like fragments of a memory long forgotten returning piece by piece. Certain insights arrived during reflection, others during moments of stillness, others still when I was not searching at all. The Work introduced itself the way true inner teachings often do: with gentleness, constancy, and a quiet certainty that it was meant to unfold not be forced.

I did not begin writing The Silent Work to teach, persuade, or impress. I began because remaining silent about what was forming within me became impossible. There are experiences that the heart understands long before the mind does, and when they reach a certain fullness, they overflow seeking expression in a form that others may recognize within themselves. This book is the result of such an overflow. It is not a doctrine to be followed, but a reflection offered to those who feel the same subtle inner calling.

# Why This Book Exists

We live in a time where the world is loud. Voices compete to be heard, knowledge is abundant yet scattered, and many are speaking but few are truly listening especially to themselves.

Silence has become unfamiliar, even uncomfortable. Yet the most meaningful transformations do not occur in noise, but in quiet spaces where the soul is finally able to breathe.

The Silent Work is a companion for those who sense that inner stillness is not emptiness, but fullness. For those who are beginning to notice that growth does not only happen through doing, but through being. For those who feel the subtle inner shift toward awareness, authenticity, and the rebuilding of the inner world.

This book does not ask you to abandon your path, beliefs, or life as it is. It invites you to enter the inner room of your own being with openness -

to explore what arises when you meet yourself without filters, masks, or performance. It is not a guide to becoming someone new, but an invitation to remember who you are beneath everything the world has layered upon you.

## How to Read This Book

There are two voices woven through these pages two ways of seeing, two doors to the same inner space.

The first is veiled: written in symbolic language, poetic imagery, and metaphor. It speaks to the intuitive, experiential, and contemplative part of you. This layer is not meant to be decoded with logic alone, but felt. Allow it to move through you like music. Some passages may reveal their meaning instantly; others may unfold only after life itself gives you the key. This is intentional.

The second is unveiled: a clear, grounded reflection that follows the veiled text. It brings the essence into everyday understanding, so that the message is not lost to mystery. This layer is not meant to remove the depth, but to bridge it - so that what is sensed may also be integrated. It provides clarity without diminishing the sacred.

Both are needed. One softens the heart; the other steadies the mind. One speaks to the soul; the other gives the soul language.

Both voices are meant to be experienced together - one revealing the inner shape of the Work, the other giving it form. Read each veiled passage, then its unveiled reflection, and allow the Gate that follows to root the insight in your lived experience. Each step builds upon the last, and together they carry you deeper into the Work.

## The Role of the Gates

### The Veiled, the Unveiled, and the Gates

After each veiled and unveiled pair, you will find a Gate. These sections are not additional commentary - they are thresholds. Each one marks a shift, a moment when the inner and outer teachings meet and open into practice.

The veiled chapters act as keys of awakening. They speak in symbols, rhythm, and silence to stir something deep within you—something older than thought and more intimate than belief. They do not ask you to understand; they ask you to remember.

The unveiled chapters act as keys of understanding.

They take what the inner self has already absorbed and give it shape, language, and clarity. They help the intellect recognize what the soul has already touched.

When both keys are turned—inner recognition through the veiled chapter, and clear comprehension through the unveiled chapter - the Gate opens.

The Gates are the places where the Work becomes living.

They take what was stirred and what was understood and lead it into embodiment. They offer reflection, slowing, and gentle practice so the insight does not remain inspiration alone.

Each Gate is a pause in the journey.

A moment for the reader to breathe, to settle, and to let the Work move from idea to identity.

For this reason, it is important not to rush. Read each veiled chapter, its unveiled companion, and the Gate that follows as one complete step. Together they ensure that you do not merely learn this Work but become it, one breath, one realization, one Gate at a time.

## A Gentle Invitation

I offer this book to you with humility and respect. Not as one who has mastered the path, but as one who has walked it sincerely enough to know its value. If you choose to turn these pages slowly, allowing the silence between the words to speak, you may find that the Work meets you exactly where you are.

You do not need to agree with everything you read. You do not need to force insight. Simply bring yourself as you are - without performance, without expectation. Let the words be a mirror. Let the silences between them become your teacher.

If at any moment something within you stirs, pauses, resists, softens, or awakens - stay with it.

That is the Work.

You are not asked to believe this book. You are only invited to experience it.

Welcome to The Silent Work.

May these pages accompany you gently as you turn inward, not to escape the world, but to meet yourself more fully within it.

— Knowledge King

THE
SILENT WORK

# Tables of Contents


**Preface 3**

How to Read This Book • Roles of the Gates • A Gentle Invitation

## The Path of the Silent Work 15

## Chapter I The Voice in the Silence  19

The Threshold of Turning Inward • The Fire Beneath the Noise • The Descent into the Shadow • The Hidden Labor of the Heart • On the Nature of Resistance • The Law of Inner Correspondence • The Emergence of the Inner Light • A Word to the Reader • Closing Reflection

## Chapter II Understanding the Inner Voice 29

The Simplicity of the Inner Path • The Lower and Higher Self Explained • What It Means to Listen • The Purpose of Struggle • The Meaning of Transformation • Closing Words

**Gate I: Bridging the Inner and Outer 37**

I. The Truth You Have Avoided • II. The Identity You Cling To • III. The Silence You Fear • IV. The Change You Resist • Seal of the First Gate

**Light Practice: Before Entering Chapter III 44**

## Chapter III The Fire and the Mirror 47

The Mirror of Light • The Fire That Transforms • The Trial of Seeing • The Voice of the Inner Flame • The Surrender • The Birth of Clarity • The Silence After Fire • Closing Reflection

## Chapter IV Living as the Light  57

From Experience to Practice • Living Between Silence and Sound • Relationships as Mirrors • Emotion and the Returning Waves • Work, Money, and the Outer World • The Discipline of Return • Signs of Inner Maturity • The Service of Presence • Closing Reflection

**Gate II The Gate of the Second Fire 64**

Seal One – The Opening of the Second Gate • Seal Two – The Fire That Refines the Seeker • Seal Three – The Turning Within and the Passage Forward • Seal of the Second Gate

**Light Practice: Before Entering Chapter V 73**

## Chapter V The Hidden Garden 75

The Soil Beneath the Mind • The Language of the Garden • The Night of the Garden • The Gardener and the Sun • The Whisper Beneath the Roots • The Communion of Mind and Spirit • The Law of Return • Closing Reflection

# Chapter VI The Mind Between Worlds 85

The Three Layer of the Mind • The Roles of Awareness • The Subconscious in Motion • The Power of Intention • The Superconscious: The Light Above the Mind • Balancing the Three • The Mind as a Sacred Instrument • Closing Reflection

**Gate III   92**

Seal One – You Can No Longer Pretend Not to Know • Seal Two – Your Choices Reveal What You Truly Serve • Seal Three – You Don't Go Back After This

**Gate III Practice: The Alignment Loop 102**

Step 1: Morning Alignment • Step 2: Midday Check-In • Step 3: End-of-Day Accountability • Step 4: Weekly Reset • How This Practice Works • If You Miss a Day • Closing Reminder for Gate III

# Chapter VII The Marriage of the Two Lights 109

The Light That Sees and the Light That Feels • The Longing of Separation • The Chamber of Union • The Dissolving of the Self • The Birth of the Living Flame • The Law of Harmony • The Unveiling of the Work • The Eternal Silence

# Chapter VIII The Union Within: Living Wholeness 117

The Two Sides of the Self • The Meaning of Inner Union • The Process of Transformation • The Heart as the Center of the Work • Recognizing Wholeness in Daily Life • The End of the Inner War • Living as a Whole Being • The Real Meaning of "The Work" • Living the Union • Closing Reflection

**Gate IV Where the Two Become One 126**

Seal One - The First Voice Appears • Seal Two - The Soft Recognition of Wholeness • Seal Three - Living Wholeness in Real Moments • Seal Four - Wholeness as Identity

**Gate IV Practice: The Meeting Within 139**

1. Entering the Heart • 2. Becoming Present to Yourself • 3. Softening Into Wholeness • 4. The Inner Union • 5. The Recognition • 6. Sealing the Inner Shift • 7. Returning With Wholeness • Closing Reflection of Gate IV

# Chapter IX The Radiance of Being 145

The Light That No Longer Seeks • The Breath Between Worlds • The World as Reflection • The Quiet Influence • The Simplicity After the Fire • The Endless Continuation • The Light That Walks

# Chapter X Living the Radiance 151

Presence in the World • Relationships as Mirrors • Work as Worship • Challenges as Teachers • The Power of Gentle Influence • Integration as Ongoing Practice • Closing Reflection
**Gate V The Return To Presence 155**
The One Behind Your Thoughts • A Familiar Presence • When Presence Begins to Reveal Itself • A Glimpse of the Real • When Presence Begins to Live Through You • The Return to Simplicity
**The Practice: Returning to Presence 164**
**Closing Silence 167**

# Chapter XI The Silence Beyond Silence 169

The Vanishing Point • The Ocean Without Shore • The Return • The Light Beyond Form • The Eternal Rest

# Chapter XII The Continuation 175

Living After the Work • Nothing to Prove • The Quiet Flow of Purpose • The Gentle Rhythm of Return • Becoming the Silence • Closing Reflection
**Gate VI: Returning to Being Human 179**
Seal One — Integration • Seal Two — The Seal • Seal of the Gate • Part A: One-Time Deep Practice - "Setting Down the Robe" • Part B: Daily Reinforcement - "The Ordinary Breath"

# Chapter XIII The Veil and the Two Natures** 185

The Language of Symbols • The Language of Clarity • Piercing the Veil • The Two Natures • The Purpose of the Structure • The Roles of the Gates • The Language of Symbols • The Flame • The Water • The Fire • The Garden • The Mirror • The Two Lights • The Silence • The Circle • The Light and the Shadow • The Soul (Consciousness) • The Spirit (Breath) • The Silence Between Symbols

# Author's Reflection 199

How the Work Found Me • The Fire That Grows in Silence

# About Knowledge King 204

# The Path of the Silent Work

*"Know thyself, and thou shalt know the universe and the Gods."*

*— Ancient Maxim*

The writings that follow are the result of years of quiet study, contemplation, and inner experience. They were not born from imagination, nor gathered from a single path or school, but drawn from the deep well of ancient wisdom that reveals itself to the earnest seeker.

Through the study of many esoteric texts, I began to recognize a hidden current connecting them all, a wisdom older than any name or order, alive in every tradition that has ever sought to awaken the divine within man. Over time, this wisdom ceased to be theory. It became an experience, a living fire that reshaped how I perceived myself and the world.

I did not set out to write a book; the book began to write itself through the transformation taking place within me. What you will read here is not a system to be believed, but a journey to be lived.

Throughout these pages, the word "soul" is used as a synonym for consciousness. This is not the consciousness of surface awareness, but the deeper light that perceives, moves, and gives life to all things. To speak of the soul is to speak of that silent essence that watches even our thoughts. It cannot be grasped by intellect alone; it must be experienced.

The intellect may point toward it, but only stillness reveals it. The transformation described herein is the sacred process of moving from the lower self to the higher from the domain of desire and impulse to the realm of wisdom and peace.

The lower self is governed by craving, fear, and the endless pursuit of gratification. It lives in reaction to the outer world, mistaking motion for purpose and noise for life.

The higher self, by contrast, moves in silence. It is

governed only by consciousness, pure awareness free of ego's distortions. To rise from one to the other is not to deny the human experience, but to refine it. The lower self is the raw material; the higher self, the perfected expression.

Through patience, discipline, and sincere introspection, the scattered fragments of being begin to unify under the guidance of consciousness. This is the silent work invisible to the world, but felt deeply in the heart.

The teachings in these pages do not seek to instruct, but to awaken recognition. Every truth written here already exists within you. My words are only a mirror, reflecting what your own inner light has always known. If you approach them with humility and a quiet mind, they may stir remembrance.

May this work serve as a guide for those who seek transformation not through belief, but through experience; not through argument, but through silence.

# Chapter I
# The Voice in the Silence

There comes a moment in every seeker's life when the outer noise grows unbearable when the opinions of others, the race of time, and the illusions of the world collapse into a single, hollow echo. It is in that echo that the soul begins to hear itself. I did not set out to become anything more than what I already was; yet something ancient stirred within me, something older than my name or my memories.

It called not from above, but from within a whisper wrapped in stillness, bidding me to remember. The more I turned toward it, the more

I realized that silence was not emptiness, but a presence living, vast, and intelligent.

## The Threshold of Turning Inward

The first step of inner transformation is not taken with the feet but with surrender. To turn inward is to descend into one's own depths, where light and shadow mingle like mist. There, the fragments of the self begin to rearrange under a silent law, a law that needs no prophet, no creed, no priest. It is written in the breath, in the pulse, in the movement of awareness itself.

Most of humanity spends its life trying to escape this descent. We build identities upon shifting ground, believing that our outer achievements can silence the inner hunger. Yet the voice within grows louder the longer it is ignored. Eventually, the soul demands attention, and life conspires to bring us back to ourselves through conflict, disappointment, or loss. When I first faced myself, I expected serenity; instead I found turbulence. I discovered how much of my strength was reaction, how much of my love was possession, and how much of my faith was fear disguised as devotion. This recognition was painful yet it was also the beginning of clarity. For one cannot purify what one refuses to see.

## The Fire Beneath the Noise

Silence is not the absence of sound. It is a living current that reveals what words conceal. When the tongue stills, the heart begins to speak; and what it speaks is truth unvarnished, unadorned, but radiant. Yet few can bear it. To hear that truth is to confront every lie we have ever told ourselves about who we are. The human mind is a restless instrument, ever seeking distraction.

It fears the quiet because the quiet unmasks it. But when one dares to rest within the silence long enough, something miraculous happens: the noise begins to dissolve, and beneath it, a subtle vibration the fire of life itself begins to reveal its pattern. This fire is not external; it burns in the core of being. It is the same essence that animates all creation, the same light that glimmers in the eyes of every living thing. To feel it is to remember one's origin. To live from it is to begin the great work of transmutation where thought becomes will, and will becomes light.

# The Descent into the Shadow

In the early stages of awakening, the shadow rises with ferocity. Everything we have repressed anger, shame, fear, resentment surges to the surface, demanding to be acknowledged. It is here that many seekers turn back, mistaking this purging for failure. But the soul cannot ascend without first reclaiming what it has cast away. For me, the descent was personal. My anger was not merely an emotion; it was a signal that my inner fire had been chained to defense instead of purpose. My pain was not punishment; it was a mirror revealing where I had abandoned myself. When I ceased to judge these forces and instead invited them to speak, they transformed. Anger became energy, pain became compassion, and what once seemed dark revealed itself as unrefined light. The silence teaches this: that darkness is not evil but unawakened power. When consciousness touches it with understanding, it turns to gold.

## The Hidden Labor of the Heart

This is the silent work: the labor that no one sees, the purification that happens in the unseen chambers of the soul. It does not require temples or rituals, though these may serve as symbols. The true temple is consciousness itself; its altar, the heart; its offering, the daily act of awareness. In the still moments of reflection, when breath slows and thought quiets, a dialogue begins between the human and the divine. It is not heard with the ears but felt with the entire being a communion beyond words. One realizes that the journey is not about reaching heaven, but about revealing it within. Every thought purified, every emotion balanced, every motive made selfless these are the unseen bricks of the inner temple. The work is patient and often lonely. The world praises achievement but seldom honors transformation. Yet those who persist discover a peace that no praise can equal.

## On the Nature of Resistance

Transformation rarely proceeds gently. The moment one commits to inner truth, life begins to test that commitment. Old habits rise in rebellion, relationships shift, and circumstances seem to conspire against the soul's progress. But this opposition is the friction that sharpens awareness. I once believed my challenges came from others that the people around me were obstacles to my peace. But life has shown me that every external conflict reflects an inner imbalance.

Those who seem to oppose us are mirrors revealing the places we are still bound. When this is understood, the struggle becomes sacred. Each difficulty, each misunderstanding, each betrayal is part of the refining process. The world itself becomes a crucible in which the soul is tempered into strength and compassion.

# The Law of Inner Correspondence

There exists a silent correspondence between the inner and outer worlds. What we harbor in thought and emotion manifests, not always as literal events, but as energetic patterns shaping the quality of our lives. The ancient sages expressed this as, "As within, so without." To master oneself is therefore to realign with the hidden order of the universe. When the heart is pure, the outer world begins to reflect harmony. When the mind is chaotic, chaos appears without. The true student of the silent work learns to read both realms as one living book. Every experience, pleasant or painful, becomes instruction. Every encounter becomes initiation. Nothing is wasted, for the unseen law uses all things to bring the soul into remembrance of its own divinity.

# The Emergence of the Inner Light

There comes a point when the work, long practiced in darkness, begins to bear fruit. One notices subtle shifts, a gentler thought, a softer word, a spontaneous act of kindness. The inner light begins to radiate naturally, without effort. This light is not for display; it is for service. It heals without intention and teaches without speech. The one who carries it walks quietly through the world, touching it with invisible grace. Such a person becomes a living sanctuary, a vessel through which higher life flows. The silence then ceases to be an exercise; it becomes a state of being. The seeker no longer needs to withdraw from the world to find peace. Peace follows them like a fragrance, emanating from the harmony within.

## A Word to the Reader

If you have found these words, it is not by accident. Something in you recognizes this path, for the silent work calls only to those who are ready. You may not yet know what awaits you, few ever do but if you feel the stirring of remembrance, honor it. Do not expect perfection; expect sincerity. Do not seek to escape the world; seek to understand it. For every stone upon your path reveals a lesson, and every shadow hides a key. The answers you seek awaken from within, not from beyond. The task is to unveil it, patiently, courageously, and in silence. The voice you seek is already speaking. It has been with you since the beginning, calm, unwavering, eternal. Listen not with your ears but with your being. Its words are simple: Be still, and know.

## Closing Reflection

I write not as a master, but as one who has been broken open by the mystery and slowly rebuilt by grace. If these words reach you, it is because the same flame that burns in me burns also in you. The journey ahead will not be easy, but it will be true. And truth once awakened never sleeps again.

# The Silent Work

# Chapter II
# Understanding the Inner Voice

The first chapter spoke in symbols of silence, of the soul, of an unseen fire working within us. This chapter is meant to clarify what those words truly mean. I want you to see that what seems mysterious is, in truth, simple. The deeper teachings of life are always simple; it is the mind that makes them complicated.

## The Simplicity of the Inner Path

The "Voice in the Silence" I wrote about is not something supernatural. It is not a voice that speaks in thunder or prophecy. It is the quiet knowing that appears when the noise of thought and emotion begins to calm. Every person has experienced this, even if they didn't name it. It's the sudden calm after confusion, the quiet certainty that says, "This is right," or, "Go this way."

It's the feeling that remains when you stop trying to control everything and simply allow yourself to be. This inner voice does not argue, rush, or repeat itself. It speaks once, gently. If you miss it, it waits. It does not use words but feeling a vibration of peace, a simple knowing. That is the true "voice in the silence."When you first begin to listen, it may be faint because the mind is loud. The mind speaks in thoughts, but the soul speaks in awareness. To hear it, you must stop chasing noise. You do not have to make the voice louder you only have to become quiet enough to recognize it.

## The Lower and Higher Self Explained

Many teachings speak of the lower self and higher self, as if they are two beings. In truth, they are two levels of one consciousness. The lower self is the part of you that reacts to the personality that wants, fears, compares, and protects. It is the self that feels separate, fragile, and constantly in need of proof (Ego). It serves a purpose: it allows us to live in the material world, to build, to survive, to experience. But when it becomes the master, life becomes restless and heavy.

The higher self is awareness itself, the quiet witness behind all experience. It is the "you" that never changes, the part that observes your moods, decisions, and thoughts without being any of them. It is pure consciousness, untouched by fear or desire. The goal is not to destroy the lower self but to bring it under the light of the higher. Think of the lower self as a child: emotional, curious, sometimes selfish but not evil. The higher self is the loving parent, patient and firm. When the parent leads, the child learns peace. When the child tries to lead, confusion follows. This is the real transformation not the death of the lower self, but its education under the guidance of consciousness.

# What It Means to Listen

To listen to the inner voice means learning to observe without rushing to fix or judge. When you are hurt, you watch the pain instead of immediately reacting. When you are angry, you notice the heat rising within instead of throwing it outward. That moment of awareness that tiny pause is the silent work. It is the place where choice is born. Before awareness, emotion controls you.

Within awareness, you begin to govern emotion. You may notice that sometimes life gives you the same problem over and over. This is not punishment. It is repetition for understanding.

The lesson will repeat until you can face it with calmness rather than reaction. Once consciousness learns, the pattern dissolves. Listening is not passive. It is the most powerful form of action. Through it, you begin to hear what life has been saying to you all along.

# The Purpose of Struggle

Many wonder why, once they begin to seek peace, life becomes more difficult. But peace is not found by escaping struggle, it is found within it.

The "fire" mentioned in the first chapter is not a physical flame; it is the heat of growth. When you commit to truth, everything false begins to surface. Old emotions rise, unhealed wounds return, relationships change. It may seem as if you are losing stability, but you are actually being cleansed. The purpose of this inner fire is to reveal what has been hidden to show you where you have been clinging to illusions.

Each challenge is like metal meeting flame: what is weak burns away, and what is true remains. If you remember this, you will stop fearing discomfort. You will understand that every difficulty is shaping you into clarity. The path of transformation is not about seeking suffering, but about not wasting it. When pain comes, ask, "What is this teaching me?".

That question turns struggle into gold.

# The Meaning of Transformation

Transformation is often imagined as becoming something greater. In truth, it is remembering what you already are beneath the noise. The higher self is not built, it is uncovered. The more you remove what is false, the more what is true shines through. You do not have to chase enlightenment. The light is already in you. What you must do is clear the fog that hides it. That fog is fear, pride, self-doubt, and the endless need to control life.

As awareness deepens, your reactions begin to change. You forgive more easily. You speak more gently. You care without losing yourself. These are signs that the higher self is leading. The ego always wants results; consciousness seeks understanding. The ego shouts, "When will I arrive?" Consciousness whispers, "You are already home."

# Closing Words

You are not alone in this journey. The same intelligence that guides the stars moves within your breath. The same light that shaped the universe glows quietly behind your thoughts. When you trust this, peace begins to grow without reason. Walk gently, observe often, speak little, and act from love.

*That is the beginning of wisdom. And wisdom, once awakened, never sleeps again.*

# *Gate I: Bridging the Inner and Outer*

Pause here.

You have passed through the first veil and its unveiling.

You tasted the Silence in symbol, and then met its meaning revealed.

Do not move forward quickly. A threshold has formed around you.

The first chapter spoke to the hidden part of your being, the place that remembers what you forgot.

The second chapter spoke to your understanding,

The part that tries to shape meaning with the mind.

But neither remembrance nor understanding is enough on its own.

Here, between these two ways of seeing,

The work begins.

Breathe once.

Not to calm yourself, but to arrive.

Let your awareness settle into the center of your being.

A quiet shift happened as you read maybe subtle, maybe stirring.

A door opened inside you.

Stand before it without rushing.

You now stand at the First Gate of the Silent Work.

This Gate is not outside of you; it rises from within.

And before you step through it,

Four truths appear not as obstacles,

But as the first teachers of the inner path.

## I. The Truth You Have Avoided

There is a part of you that has turned away from yourself.

You have filled the silence with noise,

covered your pain with movement,

and used distraction to blur what the heart has

long wanted to speak.

The Silence you met in the first chapter was not a comfort

It was a mirror.

It showed you the place you keep hidden, even from yourself.

Do not turn from it now.

Whatever you refuse to face becomes the architect of your suffering.

Whatever you are willing to meet dissolves its own power.

## II. The Identity You Cling To

Awakening cannot occur while you cling tightly to who you think you are.

The lower self the personality, the ego, the mask

Has shaped your life for many years.

It has convinced you that it is you.

But you have now felt the presence that lives behind it

The witness, the quiet awareness that does not panic,

Does not demand, does not beg to be seen.

It simply is.

You cannot carry the old identity into the inner chambers.

Something must be surrendered

Not your humanity,

But your illusions.

## III. The Silence You Fear

You say you desire peace,

yet you resist the one thing that gives it.

Silence.

Not the absence of sound

But the presence of your own being.

You fear it because silence strips away the distractions

That shields you from yourself.

It reveals what you feel.

It exposes what you believe.

It shows you where you have abandoned yourself.

But Silence is not empty.

It is full,

Alive, watchful, deep.

It is where the soul finally has room to speak.

Stay with it even when your mind protests,

When emotion rises,

When the ego trembles.

Stay.

The Silence is not your enemy

It is the path home.

## IV. The Change You Resist

You cannot step into Chapter III carrying the same patterns that carried you into Chapter I.

Already, life has pressed on the parts of you that are unhealed.

Already, the Work has begun reshaping you.

Do not mistake this pressure for punishment.

It is preparation.

What resists must soften.

What clings must loosen.

Transformation is not about gaining anything.

It is about releasing what is not you.

The Self emerges when the false falls away.

Let these four truths move through you

Not as judgment,

But as initiation.

This Gate is not here to shame you.

It is here to prepare you

To bring you into a more honest relationship with yourself,

To help you carry what you have realized in silence

Into the way you think, act, breathe, and choose.

If you feel tension inside you

Part awakening, part resisting

Good.

Tension is the threshold.

You are not meant to remove it.

You are meant to walk through it.

Understand this:

The veiled chapter revealed the mystery.

The unveiled chapter revealed the meaning.

This Gate now demands integration.

You are no longer reading about Silent Work.

You have entered it.

Do not cross into Chapter III as the same person who began Chapter I.

Let something inside you shift, even something small:

A softening, a surrender, a willingness to see yourself clearly.

This is not a chapter to learn.

It is a threshold to cross.

Only when the inner begins to shape the outer does the Work truly begin.

## *Seal of the First Gate*

To move forward without aligning your inner and outer is to carry an unopened gift into the next room.
Pause.
Integrate.
Continue only when you are with yourself.

**Light Practice: Before Entering Chapter III**
*Do this once before reading Chapter III.*
*It takes only minutes, but it marks the crossing.*

**1.** Sit where you are.
Let the body grow still.

**2.** Close your eyes.
Let the world fall gently to the edges.

**3.** Breathe once.
Not to calm but to arrive.

**4.** Place your awareness in the center of your chest. No imagery. No forcing. Just presence.

**5.** Ask inwardly, "What truth about myself am I now willing to stop running from?"
Do not search.
Do not dig.
Let it rise.

**6.** Whisper within yourself,
"I am willing to change."
Not "I am ready."
Not "I know how."

Just Willingness.

## When the moment feels complete, open your eyes.
## This is your crossing.
## Now, you may continue.

# Chapter III
# The Fire and the Mirror

*"Only when the flame turns inward does it learn
that it was light all along."*

There is a place within where the soul is shown its own face. Not the one the world knows, not the smile, the name, or the story but the one that has watched from behind the eyes since the beginning. It waits, patient and eternal, for the moment when the seeker is ready to see. At first, the mirror was dark. The light of consciousness has not yet reached its surface. We sense it there silent, hidden but dare not look. We fear what may appear, for to see truth is to lose every illusion that once protected us. Yet the mirror cannot be avoided forever. The path leads all who walk it to that still threshold where self meets Self, and fire begins its holy work.

# The Mirror of Light

I once believed the mirror of the soul would reveal only beauty. I thought it would show the perfection I sought. But when the veil lifted, it revealed everything I had hidden every shadow, every wound, every neglected truth. It was not cruel; it was complete. The mirror does not flatter; it reveals. It shows light and darkness without judgment, for both belong to the whole. When you stand before it, there is no pretense, no mask, no defense. It reflects not what you pretend to be, but what you are. In that moment, I saw the restless patterns of my lower nature: desires chasing desires, fears wrapped in pride, anger disguised as strength. I saw the part of me that wanted love yet feared it, that longed for truth yet resisted change. The mirror showed me not my failures, but my fragments. It showed me the scattered pieces of a self I had tried to forget. And beneath them faint but unmistakable I saw light.

## The Fire That Transforms

As I gazed upon that light, a warmth arose from within. It was not the warmth of comfort, but of purification. The light became fire, not one that burned the flesh, but one that burned falsehood. Every untrue thought began to tremble. Every selfish motive turned to ash. Every mask I had worn melted into transparency. The fire asked nothing but honesty. It consumed nothing real, only the illusions I clung to for safety. I realized the flames were not punishing me; they were freeing me. They were the living intelligence of consciousness, the same light that formed stars now working within the human heart. Pain, I discovered, was not the enemy. It was resistance to change that caused suffering. The fire only hurts when we cling to what must pass. Once surrendered, it becomes warmth, a sacred presence that purifies without destroying. The lower self fears this process, for it believes it will die. But the higher self knows it will only awaken.

## The Trial of Seeing

The mirror grows brighter the longer one dares to look. It spares no corner of the soul. I saw my pride, the secret belief that I had already arrived. I saw my impatience, hidden beneath the mask of passion. I saw the many ways I had used ego to avoid truth. And in seeing these things, I was given a choice: to turn away, or to remain. To remain is the true trial. For the ego, revelation feels like death. It seeks to defend, to justify, to explain. But the mirror does not argue. It only reflects. In that stillness, I understood that nothing seen is to be hated. Every shadow is a part of the journey, the unrefined aspect of a greater light. The same power that creates the sun hides within the night. I whispered within myself, "Let the light do its work." And the fire answered, "I already am."

# The Voice of the Inner Flame

Then came a silence unlike any before, not empty, but filled with presence. Within it, I heard a voice, not from without, but from within the very flame.

*It Said*:

You cannot purify what you still condemn.

You cannot rise while holding the weight of self-judgment.

The shadow you fear is your own light, seen from another angle.

I listened, and the words became revelation.

To see is to forgive. To forgive is to be free. To be free is to remember.

I realized that consciousness is not a war between opposites, but a marriage of them.

The lower and higher selves are not enemies, they are two halves of the same divine polarity.

The fire exists to unite them.

# The Surrender

When I could no longer bear the weight of what I saw, something in me broke quietly, gently, like ice under sunlight. It was not destruction, but release. I felt myself falling into something vast and loving. There was no more effort, no more striving. I did not know what I was becoming, only that I was no longer who I had been. The mirror dissolved. The fire softened. All that remained was stillness, radiant, conscious stillness. In that stillness, I felt no boundary between myself and life. The world, once divided into "me" and "them," "light" and "dark," "past" and "future," merged into one endless now. The silence had become a voice, and the voice had become light.

# The Birth of Clarity

When the fire faded, I did not return as the same being. Something subtle had shifted. I noticed that my thoughts moved slower, my words carried weight, and my heart no longer hurried to judge. I could look upon my own shadow without fear. I could look upon others and see not opposition, but mirrors of my own lessons. The mirror had not vanished; it had moved inside. It now reflected every moment of life back to me, asking only one question: "Will you stay awake?"

I understood then that purification is not a single event, but an eternal process. The fire burns gently every day, refining thought, word, and deed. And the more one yields to it, the more luminous life becomes. Clarity is not perfection; it is presence. It is seeing clearly without fleeing. It is loving what is true enough to let it change you.

## The Silence After Fire

There is a silence after fire that cannot be described as a quiet that is both empty and full. It is the silence of consciousness resting in itself, no longer seeking. In that silence, the soul realizes it was never lost, only asleep. The mirror and the fire were never external. They were symbols of what was happening within consciousness recognizing itself as light through the act of awareness. And now, when I look at others, I see the same process unfolding each person standing before their own mirror, each flame uniquely shaped by their path. Some resist, some surrender, but all are moving toward the same remembrance. The fire is universal. The mirror is eternal. The work is the same.

## Closing Reflection

The path does not end here; it deepens. After the fire, the soul must learn to live as light to walk in the world without forgetting its source.

This is where the silent work becomes life itself. The flame continues, but it no longer burns. It illuminates.

There is a peace beyond reward, a joy beyond reason, a love that asks for nothing.

When this awakens, one no longer seeks the divine... one is it, expressed in human form.

In this realization, the seeker vanishes, and only awareness remains watching, loving, being.

And in that eternal stillness, the voice whispers once more:

*"You are the mirror, you are the fire, you are the light that sees itself."*

# The Silent Work

# Chapter IV
# Living as the Light

When the inner fire quiets and clarity begins to form, the next step is learning how to live from that light. Illumination is not an ending, it is a beginning. The silent work does not remove us from the world; it teaches us how to move through it differently. Many people think awakening should make life perfect. But awakening does not erase responsibility, emotion, or challenge. It simply changes the way we meet them. Instead of reacting from fear, we begin to respond from awareness. The same situations appear, yet the way we see them transforms everything.

# From Experience to Practice

The light revealed in silence must become a
way of living. It does not ask for grand gestures
or new beliefs, only consistency. What you
discovered in stillness must now guide your
speech, your choices, and your relationships. Each
day gives countless opportunities to practice.
When you feel impatience rising, breathe and
remember the fire of that moment of seeing truth
without defense. When someone misunderstands
you, remember the mirror how every encounter
reflects something waiting to be understood.
When you feel the pull of old habits, pause.
Do not condemn yourself. Awareness itself is
a correction. This is how inner work becomes
outer life: by returning, again and again, to
consciousness before reaction.

# Living Between Silence and Sound

You cannot remain in meditation forever. Life
requires movement, conversation, and decision.
The lesson is to carry silence into those moments
to speak from it, act from it, and think within it.

Silence does not mean withdrawal; it means presence. When you listen fully before speaking, you are practicing silence. When you give attention without judgment, you are practicing silence. When you move deliberately instead of rushing, you are practicing silence. True silence is not the absence of sound; it is the absence of unconsciousness.

## Relationships as Mirrors

After awakening, relationships often change. Some fade, some deepen, some challenge you more than before. This is natural. When you change vibration, life rearranges to match it. The key is not to judge others for where they are, nor to feel superior for what you see. Everyone stands before their own mirror. Compassion grows when you remember this. Instead of trying to fix people, embody peace. Instead of convincing others, live the truth quietly. Your presence will teach more than words ever could. The higher self does not argue it radiates.

# Emotion and the Returning Waves

Even after illumination, emotions will still come. Light does not destroy the tide; it teaches you to surf it. Sadness, anger, desire these are natural forces. The difference is that now you can feel them without losing yourself in them. They become messages instead of masters. When sadness appears, it might be asking for rest. When anger arises, it may reveal where a boundary was crossed. When desire grows strong, it may point toward an unexpressed part of your potential. The task is not to suppress emotion but to listen to it consciously. Each feeling carries information. Awareness turns that information into wisdom.

# Work, Money, and the Outer World

Spiritual awareness is not separate from practical life. Earning a living, caring for family, creating, building these too are expressions of the higher self when done with integrity and attention. Bring consciousness into your work. Focus on quality, not quantity. Let your actions serve life rather than ego. Even simple tasks, done with awareness, become sacred. Money itself is neutral. It becomes pure when used with purpose, or poisonous when pursued for power. The measure is not what you have but how consciously you handle it. The silent work is not a retreat from the material, it is its sanctification.

## The Discipline of Return

No matter how awakened you feel, you will drift. The mind will pull you back into distraction, pride, or old emotion. This is not failure. It is rhythm. Awareness expands and contracts like breath. The practice is to return without shame, without story. Each time you remember to be conscious, the flame brightens. Each time you forgive yourself for forgetting, you strengthen humility. Progress is not measured by how long you stay awake, but by how gently you return when you fall asleep.

# Signs of Inner Maturity

You will know the light is stabilizing when:

- You react slower and listen longer.

- You can be misunderstood without the need to defend.

- You feel peace even when things are uncertain.

- Gratitude arises without reason.

- You desire less and appreciate more.

# The Service of Presence

As consciousness matures, love becomes its natural language. Not sentimental love, but the quiet radiance of understanding. You will notice that your very presence begins to affect others. Without trying, you bring calm where there was tension, clarity where there was confusion. This is service without effort. It does not require titles or recognition. Simply by being true to the light within, you become a channel for healing. The world does not need more teachers; it needs more examples of awareness in action.

# Closing Reflection

Illumination is not an escape from humanity; it is the fulfillment of it. To live as the light is to be fully awake, kind, and free. You will still stumble, but you will stumble consciously. You will still feel pain, but you will no longer be ruled by it. You will still walk through darkness, but now with the lamp of understanding in your hand. The silent work continues quietly behind every smile, every breath, every act of compassion. It is not something you perform, it is what you are becoming. Remember: awareness is not achieved; it is revealed, moment by moment, through living. When life is lived consciously, the ordinary becomes sacred, and every heartbeat whispers the oldest truth:

*"You are the light that life uses to see itself."*

# Gate II: The Gate of the Second Fire

## The Fire That Becomes Life**

## Seal One – The Opening of the Second Gate

Pause here.

Do not move lightly across this threshold.

The mirror revealed what was hidden.

The fire showed what cannot remain.

Both brought you closer to yourself than you have ever allowed.

Now, a quieter turning begins

A shift not of vision, but of being.

The first Gate awakened recognition.

The unveiling brought understanding.

But knowledge alone cannot carry you further.

The Work now asks something deeper:

To live from what you have seen.

You may feel the pull of two directions within you.

The clarity touched in silence,

And the habits that wait to reclaim their place.

This tension is not a flaw.

It is the sign that you stand between worlds.

The question before you is no longer, "Can I see?"

You have already seen.

The question now is,

"Will I choose what I have seen?"

Breathe once.

Let the truth settle inside you.

To continue without grounding yourself in the Light you glimpsed

Would be to carry an unopened truth into the next chamber.

The Veiled and the Unveiled must now become one movement within you.

This Gate prepares you for the second fire

Not the fire that awakens,

But the fire that reshapes.

## *Seal Two – The Fire That Refines the Seeker*

The first fire showed you your shadow.

This one shows you your mask.

Many have touched truth in silence,

only to return to their lives unchanged

still reacting, still defending, still hiding.

This Gate exists to keep you from becoming one of them.

Understand this gently:

The ego does not fear awakening.

It fears being lived beyond.

It will now reach for new disguises:

not pride, but spiritual pride.

Not identity, but a "holy" identity.

Not illusion, but the illusion of having no illusions.

The second fire reveals these subtleties.

You will know it has begun when you notice:

- a quiet judgment of those who have not awakened

- a desire to be seen as conscious or wise

- a feeling of distance from the "unaware"

- a subtle superiority

- the wish to appear transformed

Do not condemn this.

That, too, is ego.

Simply see it, the way you would see a shadow in soft light.

The moment you see it without flinching,

the fire begins to refine you again.

True light does not announce itself.

True clarity does not demand recognition.

True awakening does not require an audience.

Let this be known:

The second fire burns, not only, the darkness you

hid from, but the brightness you tried to perform.

Remain still within it.

Let the flame reveal what blocks you from transparency.

Let it strip away every image you cling to.

Not through force but through allowing.

When you stop protecting the parts that fear the flame,

The Work begins to shape you without resistance.

## Seal Three – The Turning Within and the Passage Forward

You whispered the words:

I am willing to change.

Let them echo.

Willingness is the doorway through which transformation enters.

Not mastery.

Not certainty.

Not perfection.

Willingness.

The fire now moves from your inner world into your life.

This is where clarity becomes character,

and awakening becomes embodiment.

Do not fear the rhythm that will follow:
you will rise and fall,

remember and forget,

open and contract.

This is not failure.

It is the pulse of becoming.

Each time you return to awareness,

you strengthen the witness.

Each time you soften in the fire,

you deepen humility.

Each time you respond with presence instead of reaction,

you anchor light into form.

No one sees this work but you.

There is no applause in the private corrections you make.

Yet these unseen moments shape destiny more than any public act.

A pause before speaking.

A breath before reacting.

A softening where you once hardened.

A willingness to see yourself in the other.

These are the stones of the inner temple

becoming the architecture of your life.

The Second Gate does not ask you to be perfect.

It asks you to be honest, humble, and willing as you walk.

Remember this:

Integration is not the absence of shadow.

It is the presence of light within it.

Walk gently.

Walk truthfully.

Walk with the awareness that meets each moment

as a teacher.

Let this seal rest upon you:

Do not perform the light.

Become transparent enough that the light performs itself through you.

When you feel the light moving without your interference,

you will know the Second Gate has been crossed quietly, inwardly, as though a door opened from the inside.

Take one slow inhale…

and one soft exhale.

You may now receive the Seal.

## Seal of the Second Gate

What was awakened must now be lived.

What was purified must now be expressed.

Walk forward not as one who understands, but as one who embodies.

## Light Practice: Before Entering Chapter V
*Do this once before reading Chapter V.*

1. Recall one recent moment where you forgot the light.
Not to judge. Only to see.

2. Bring awareness to it softly.
No story. No analysis.

3. Place a hand over your chest and whisper inwardly:
"I see you. You are allowed to change."

4. Breathe in through the nose.
Exhale gently through the mouth.

5. Ask inwardly:
"How would I live this moment if I remembered the light?"

6. Let the answer arise on its own as a feeling, a word, or a quiet knowing.

7. Whisper inwardly:
"I choose this."
Let the breath settle.
Let the choice register.

*When you begin Chapter V, you will not enter
as the one who read, but as the one
who is becoming.*

# The Silent Work

# Chapter V
# The Hidden Garden

There is a place within where all things take root before they are seen: a garden beneath thought, watered by emotion, tended by silence. There, the seeds of every word and feeling are planted long before the harvest of experience appears. Most walk through life unaware of this inner soil, yet everything they call "fate" grows from it. I came upon this garden not by seeking it, but by being still long enough to feel what moves beneath awareness. At first it seemed like darkness, a quiet depth with no form. But when I looked closer, I saw movement beneath the surface, like wind through unseen leaves. Something was living there ancient, obedient, and infinitely fertile.

# The Soil Beneath the Mind

The garden beneath the mind remembers everything. It keeps the fragrance of every thought ever breathed into it, the imprint of every emotion, every fear, every hope. It does not argue with the gardener; it only receives. It grows weeds and roses alike with equal devotion. I once thought I was a victim of circumstance, but the garden showed me otherwise. It whispered, "Nothing happens to you that you have not already grown within." The storms that shook my life were not punishments but harvests manifestations of forgotten seeds I had sown through worry, anger, or belief. The garden is faithful; it does not choose what to nurture. Whatever the heart plants, it brings to life.

# The Language of the Garden

This hidden place does not understand words as the tongue speaks them. Its language is feeling the vibration behind the thought, the emotion carried on the breath.

When we speak with fear, it hears fear. When we think with faith, it hears faith. It listens not to our prayers but to our state of being. Thus, the inner work is not to beg heaven for change, but to purify the voice that speaks within to make the heart calm enough that its whisper carries truth instead of confusion. The garden will mirror whatever tone we bring to it. When peace speaks, it blossoms. When conflict speaks, it hardens. And when silence speaks when no thought disturbs its soil it reveals the face of the divine gardener behind all things.

## The Night of the Garden

To enter this sacred ground is to descend into memory. There we meet not angels first, but the echoes of what we have forgotten: fears that were never released, desires that still ache, and words we once spoke against ourselves that still grow in shadow. This is the true night of the soul not a punishment, but a cleansing. The deeper we go, the more clearly we see what lives in the roots. Some of what grows there was planted by others:

a parent's fear, a friend's doubt, a society's expectation. Yet once seen, it becomes ours to uproot. Awareness is the flame that purifies the soil. It burns nothing real, only what no longer belongs.

## The Gardener and the Sun

There is a sun that shines within every human being. It is the light of pure consciousness the witness that observes all things. When that sun rises over the hidden garden, shadows lose their power. The soil, once dense with confusion, becomes luminous. Old seeds awaken as new virtues; forgotten pain transforms into wisdom. The garden does not change because we fight it, but because we illuminate it. The gardener's hands are not tools of control but of attention. Where the light of attention falls, life reorders itself in silence. It is not effort that sanctifies the ground, but awareness. Effort digs; awareness cultivates.

# The Whisper Beneath the Roots

In the stillest moments, if one listens beyond thought, a faint rhythm can be felt beneath the surface the pulse of the earth itself breathing within the soul. It is the same current that moves the tides and opens the flower. That pulse is the divine will, flowing through the hidden garden to give form to every experience. To resist it is to harden the soil. To flow with it is to let creation move freely through you. The wise learn to feel that rhythm and move as it moves. They no longer fight the seasons within themselves. They plant in patience, water with faith, and harvest in gratitude.

# The Communion of Mind and Spirit

Above the soil, thought wanders like wind. Beneath it, the living ground waits for instruction. When both are aligned the sunlight of awareness and the soil of the unseen the garden becomes a mirror of heaven itself. This union is the true marriage of mind and soul. The mind provides form; the soul provides life. The mind imagines; the soul makes real. When the two are joined in harmony, creation becomes effortless, and the world reflects inner peace as outer order. Every sage, every mystic, every awakened being has tended this same garden. Their blossoms differ, but the soil is one.

## The Law of Return

The garden forgets nothing.

Every seed will bloom in its appointed season. If you have planted fear, you will one day walk among its thorns.

If you have sown love, you will rest beneath its shade.

But mercy lives within the law.

Each new moment is fresh ground.

Every breath carries the power to plant anew.

Even the oldest field, long neglected, can be renewed by attention and light.

Forgiveness is rain upon that soil.

Gratitude is sunlight.

And silence, silence is the fertile darkness where the next creation begins.

## Closing Reflection

The hidden garden is not apart from you; it is you.

It is the unseen part of the self that listens more deeply than thought.

It is where dreams are born, where prayers take shape,

where life answers life in the secret language of vibration.

Tend it gently.

Speak to it with truth.

Let no seed fall carelessly from your lips or your mind.

For what you plant within will one day stand before you,

and what you nurture in peace will return
multiplied.

The gardener and the garden are one,

and the silent work is nothing more

than learning to remember this.

*"All things bloom in their season,
but the seed is eternal."*

# Chapter VI
# The Mind Between Worlds

The garden beneath thought is powerful, but it does not work alone. Between the hidden soil and the light of spirit stands the conscious mind the bridge between heaven and earth. It is here, in the quiet center of awareness, that two worlds meet: the world of form and the world of essence, the seen and the unseen. To understand this meeting place is to begin to master both worlds.

## The Three Layers of the Mind

Human consciousness moves through three primary layers: the conscious, the subconscious, and the superconscious.

- The conscious mind is your daily awareness, the part that chooses, reasons, and focuses.

- The subconscious is the deep memory of all experience in the inner garden that gives form to your thoughts and emotions.

- The superconscious is the higher intelligence, the divine pattern that guides evolution itself.

When these three levels work together, the human being becomes a channel for divine order in the material world. But when they are divided when the conscious mind drifts in distraction, or the subconscious is filled with fear the bridge collapses, and confusion takes its place.

The silent work teaches you how to restore this inner unity.

## The Role of Awareness

Awareness is the meeting point of all levels of mind.It observes without judgment and connects without force. When you rest in awareness, you stand in the doorway between the seen and the unseen. This is why stillness is so important. The subconscious speaks in symbols and emotion, the superconscious in inspiration and intuition. Awareness is the interpreter of both the translator of heaven's whisper into human understanding. When awareness is strong, you no longer get lost in thoughts or sensations. You begin to sense the quiet current beneath events the meaning hidden in experience. *"Awareness does not control the mind; it illuminates it."*

## The Subconscious in Motion

Every reaction, every sudden emotion, every attraction and aversion you feel in daily life is the subconscious revealing itself. It is constantly expressing the patterns planted within it. When you become conscious of this, you stop being a victim of habit and begin to observe the pattern itself. For example, if anger rises easily, it shows where the inner soil still carries roots of defense or fear. If joy arises without reason, it shows that love has begun to bloom. Observation is the key. You cannot change what you hate, but you can illuminate what you see. The moment you look at a pattern with full awareness, the old energy begins to dissolve. The garden reorders itself under the light.

## The Power of Intention

Intention is the way the conscious mind plants new seeds. Every thought charged with emotion is a command to the subconscious. When you hold a thought with steady feeling and no contradiction, the deeper mind begins to shape life to match it. But intention is not force; it is alignment. You are not ordering the subconscious you are aligning your will with the creative law already at work within it. The most powerful intention feels peaceful, not desperate.It carries faith instead of strain. The subconscious obeys the vibration of certainty. That is why prayer, visualization, or affirmation only work when the heart and mind agree.

*"The garden does not answer words; it answers atmosphere."*

# The Superconscious: The Light Above the Mind

Beyond both the conscious and the subconscious lies the superconscious, the higher awareness that whispers through intuition, beauty, and sudden clarity. It is the divine blueprint within every soul, the silent knowing of what you are meant to become. When the lower mind quiets and the subconscious is purified, this higher intelligence begins to speak clearly. It comes as insight that feels both new and ancient, as guidance that needs no proof. You may call it divine mind, higher self, or inner light names do not matter. It is the pure consciousness behind all form. The task of the conscious mind is not to reach this light but to make room for it to become transparent, receptive, and still enough that the higher current can flow through without distortion.

# Balancing the Three

The silent work aligns the three minds like instruments in a single symphony.

1. Conscious Mind: Chooses what to plant.

2. Subconscious: Nurtures and manifests the seed.

3. Superconscious: Provides the divine pattern, the energy of creation itself.

When aligned, your thoughts carry clarity, your emotions harmonize with your purpose, and your life begins to reflect inner order. You no longer fight against circumstances; you move with the rhythm of truth. When divided, confusion arises. The conscious says one thing, the subconscious feels another, and the higher guidance cannot reach through the noise. The work, therefore, is not self-perfection, but self-harmony.

## The Mind as a Sacred Instrument

When the mind is pure, it becomes transparent to spirit.

Thought no longer resists reality; it cooperates with it.

Emotion no longer clouds perception; it colors it with compassion.

The mind then becomes what it was always meant to be a bridge between worlds, a translator of infinity into time. At this stage, the seeker is no longer merely transforming they are creating consciously. Every action becomes prayer, every moment revelation.

Life itself becomes meditation.

## Closing Reflection

The silent work is the art of uniting what has always been one: the conscious gardener, the hidden garden, and the light that gives both life. When you learn to live from that unity, you discover that heaven was never a distant realm. It was the harmony between your thoughts, your heart, and your awareness. The mind, once restless, becomes a still lake reflecting the sky. And in its reflection you finally see what has been true all along:

*"You were never between worlds. You were the bridge itself."*

# Gate III

## *Seal One – You Can No Longer Pretend Not to Know*

Pause here.

Take a breath before moving forward. What you are entering now is not new information, but a new level of responsibility for what you have already learned. You have seen what grows beneath the surface of your life. You have learned that your inner world is not random, and that nothing within you is without consequence. Through the hidden garden, you discovered that every thought, feeling, belief, and repeated inner state becomes a seed that eventually shows itself in the conditions of your life. You now understand that your "fate" has roots and many of those roots were planted by your own inner climate. You have also learned that the mind is not one voice, but a layered instrument. You now know how the conscious, subconscious, and higher mind interact, and how misalignment between them creates confusion, conflict, and repeated cycles. You saw how awareness acts as the bridge, and how intention shapes the direction of the inner garden. You learned that the subconscious listens to the tone of your inner state more than your words, and that the higher mind can only be heard in stillness. These are not small realizations. They are turning points the kind that change a person's life if they choose to live by them. And now that you know these things, you can no longer pretend you don't. You can no longer say, "I don't know why this keeps happening to me," because you now understand that the conditions of your life reflect the conditions of your inner soil. You can no longer speak carelessly to yourself or about your life without knowing that your words carry weight. You can no longer claim that your reactions are "just how you are," because you now see they are long-rooted patterns surfacing for recognition. You can no longer tell yourself that your thoughts don't matter, when you have learned they are seeds. This is the threshold of Gate III:

The moment when understanding demands

embodiment. Until now, inner growth may have felt personal, reflective, and largely unseen. But once you see how the inner creates the outer, silence becomes a teacher and excuses begin to fall apart. What you choose from this point forward cannot come from habit or ignorance. It must come from awareness. This Seal is not asking you to be perfect. It is asking you to be honest. Honest about the thoughts you continue to feed. Honest about the emotions you allow to repeat without question. Honest about the stories you keep alive in your mind. Honest about the moments you betray what you know, just to stay comfortable. Knowing changes things. And once you know, pretending not to is a form of self-abandonment. This is where many people turn back not because the path becomes unclear, but because it becomes clear enough that excuses no longer hold. It is easier to say "life is happening to me" than to admit "life is responding to me." It is easier to stay unconscious than to live with awareness. Awareness brings choice, and choice brings responsibility. From this point on, the Work will expect more of you. Not more strain, more sincerity. Not more effort, more alignment. Not more intensity, more truth. Let this Seal settle in you: You now understand how your inner world creates your outer experience. From this moment forward, your life is shaped not by what you know, but by whether you live what you know.

Before you continue, take a moment of quiet.

Ask yourself:

"Where in my life am I still acting as if I do not know the truth I have already seen?"

Do not rush to answer.
Let the question sit with you, even if it feels uncomfortable.

Clarity will come, and when it does, something in you will be unable to go back to the old way of living.

## Seal Two – Your Choices Reveal What You Truly Serve

You now understand how the inner world shapes

the outer. Seal One made something clear:
once you see the mechanics of your inner life,
pretending not to see them is a choice.

## *"This Seal is about that choice."*

Because it is easy to speak about inner work, to
reflect, to journal, to "be aware," and still return
to the same habits, the same reactions, the same
self-betrayal. It is easy to know and not live.
And if you refuse to live what you know, then
knowledge becomes another disguise, another
way to avoid change while appearing to seek it.
Here is the truth, without decoration: Your life is
built on what you choose, not what you intend.
Your patterns, relationships, behavior, tone,
reactions, boundaries, standards, speech, and daily
decisions show exactly who is leading your life
awareness or habit. You can talk about growth,
but if your choices contradict what you claim to
know, then growth is not what you are serving.
You are serving comfort. You are serving fear.
You are serving the familiar pattern you refuse to
release. Awareness that does not change how you
live is not awareness, it is avoidance with better

language. Look at your life honestly: If you understand the hidden garden yet continue planting with negativity, self-doubt, resentment, or careless thought, then you are choosing your own weeds. If you understand how the subconscious follows your inner tone, yet still feed it with self-criticism, drama, or imagined worst-case scenarios, then you are choosing to poison your own soil. If you understand the role of the conscious mind, yet keep choosing what you know weakens you, drains you, or betrays your values, then you are not confused, you are committed to the comfort of who you were. And if you understand the higher mind's guidance, yet ignore the quiet knowing that tells you the truth, then you are not "waiting for a sign." You are avoiding responsibility. Do not tell yourself you are "working on it" if your choices reflect surrender to the old self. Do not claim to value peace if you still choose environments, conversations, and behaviors that disturb it.

Do not say you want alignment if you repeatedly choose what pulls you out of it. Your choices are your real beliefs. Everything else is commentary. Look at how you show up with others. Look at how you speak when you're frustrated. Look at how quickly you abandon your inner center when ego wants to be fed. Look at how you justify what you know is misaligned because change feels inconvenient. This Seal asks you to remove every excuse that allows you to know better while continuing to live the same. From this point on: When you choose against what you know is true, admit the truth of that choice: You chose habit over growth. You chose fear over awareness. You chose the familiar over the honest. That level of self-honesty is where transformation begins. It is not perfection that moves you forward, it is integrity. Integrity means your actions match your understanding. Where they don't, you correct yourself without delay, without story, and without escaping into "I'm trying." You are not asked to never fall. You are asked to stop pretending you don't know why you fell, or who did the choosing. Let this Seal confront you, but not condemn you. Its purpose is to return your power back to you because if your choices shape your life, then choosing differently is the beginning of freedom.

## *Seal Three – You Don't Go Back After This*

There is a point in inner growth where returning to who you used to be is no longer possible not because you can't, but because you can no longer do it without knowing you're abandoning yourself. This Seal marks that point. You have seen what lies beneath your thoughts. You have seen how your inner state shapes your outer life. You have seen the role your choices play in either reinforcing an old identity or building a new one. Once this level of clarity is reached, "not knowing" is no longer available as a shield. You can't unsee what you now understand. You can't unknow what creates your life. And you can't pretend your choices are accidental. This Seal is not about perfection, it is about personal truth. From here forward, you can feel when something is beneath you, when a choice contradicts your growth, when your behavior does not match your understanding. You will feel the discomfort of misalignment faster and more clearly than before.

That discomfort is not punishment, it is evidence of who you are becoming. This Seal asks you to recognize something important: You are no longer the person who is "trying to grow." You are someone who knows what growth requires. You no longer get to hide behind "I didn't realize," "I slipped without noticing," or "I wasn't aware." If you choose an old pattern now, you will feel the weight of that choice, because you will know it is a choice. That awareness is your strength, not your burden. It means you are capable of choosing differently.  Not someday, not when it's easy, but now. It means your standard for yourself has changed. It means you hold yourself to a level of honesty that does not allow you to shrink back to who you were. This Seal is the line between the old way of living and the new one.

From this point on:

• When you speak, you will know if you are speaking from truth or from habit.

• When you react, you will know if it is a conscious response or a trained pattern.

• When you make decisions, you will feel which part of you is choosing.

And because you now recognize the difference, you cannot genuinely return to unconscious living not without feeling the cost of betraying yourself.

You don't need to announce this shift to anyone. You don't need to prove it, perform it, or make it dramatic.

You simply live differently because you know differently.

This Seal is not about pressure. It is about identity.

You are stepping into the version of yourself who can no longer pretend to be unaware. The version who chooses alignment, not occasionally, but intentionally. The version who sees clearly, who takes responsibility, who adjusts when they fall, and who moves forward without excuses.

You don't go back after this, not because you're trapped, but because you're awake.

If you ever try to shrink into an old version of yourself, it will feel too small to live in. That is not failure. That is evidence of growth.

Let this Seal settle as a quiet, steady truth.

## *Gate III Practice*: *The Alignment Loop*

This practice is designed to train you to live what you know, consistently. It removes the gap between understanding and action by holding you accountable to your own awareness each day. Do it daily, morning and night, for at least seven days.

### *Step* 1: *Morning Alignment* (2 - 5 *minutes*)

Before your day begins, set your inner state. Ask yourself, out loud or in writing:

1. "Who do I choose to be today?"
(Choose one quality: calm, clear, honest, disciplined, compassionate, etc.)

2. "What does alignment look like for me today?"
(One concrete behavior that reflects who you chose to be.)

3. "What situation is most likely to pull me out of alignment?"
(Identify it now so you won't be surprised later.)

End with this grounding sentence: "I will not abandon what I know when it becomes inconvenient."

## Step 2: *Midday Check-In* (30 *seconds* – 1 *minute*)

At some point halfway through your day pause.
Ask yourself three questions:

1. Am I in alignment with who I chose to be today?

2. Which part of my day tested my alignment the most?

3 If I slipped, what is the next aligned action I can take right now?

Act immediately on the last answer.
Do not wait for a "better moment."

## Step 3: *End-of-Day Accountability* (3 – 5 *minutes*)

This step prevents self-deception, excuses, and

"I'll do better tomorrow" loops.

Answer these without softening:

1. Where did I choose in alignment today? (Name at least one moment you lived what you know.)

2. Where did I choose against what I know? (Be honest. No story, no justification.)

3. What triggered the misalignment? (Identify the real cause not the excuse.)

4. How will I choose differently next time? (One specific correction not a vague promise.)

Close your nightly reflection by reading this once: "I do not need to be perfect to grow, but I must be honest to change."

### Step 4: *Weekly Reset (Once every 7 days)*

At the end of each week, review your daily notes and complete this short reset:

1. What pattern keeps repeating?

2. What truth have I been avoiding living?

3. What is one decision I know I need to make, that I haven't made yet?

Then write this sentence:
"I know what needs to be done. I will not pretend otherwise."

This is your weekly line in the sand.

## How This Practice Works

This loop trains three essential muscles of transformation:

1. Awareness in the moment (Morning Alignment)

2. Correction during the day (Midday Check-In)

3. Honesty at the end of the day (Night Accountability)

Repeated daily, this builds identity, not through thought, but through lived integrity.

## If You Miss a Day

Do not restart. Do not punish yourself.

Return to the practice the next morning, but

include this question that night: "What excuse did I use to abandon what I know?"

Own it. Then continue.

### *Closing Reminder for Gate III*

This practice has one purpose: To remove the gap between what you know and how you live.

If you do it sincerely, without story, without loopholes, you will not be able to slip back into unconscious living without feeling the truth of it.

And feeling the truth of misalignment is what pushes you back into alignment.

# This is the Work of Gate III

*"You are someone who knows.
And because you know,
you choose differently now."*

# Chapter VII
# The Marriage of the Two Lights

There are two lights within every human being. One shines downward, seeking to illuminate the earth. The other shines upward, longing to return to its source. For lifetimes they have looked upon one another through the veil of form one calling, the other answering, yet never touching. But there comes a moment in the journey when the veil thins. The heart begins to tremble with a quiet knowing: that the two lights are not strangers, but reflections of a single flame. This moment is the beginning of the sacred union, the reconciliation of heaven and earth within the soul.

# The Light That Sees and the Light That Feels

The first light is the seer, the light of awareness that observes, chooses, and directs. It is the sun within, radiant and active, giving clarity and purpose. It names things, divides them, and brings them to order. The second is the feeler the moon within, receptive and deep. It moves not through thought but through rhythm and reflection. It holds memory, sensation, and the secret language of emotion. The two lights were never meant to be at war. Their harmony sustains the inner universe; their separation creates darkness. When the seer dominates, life becomes dry and brittle. When the feeler rules, life becomes a tide of unshaped desire. Only when they gaze into one another do they reveal the wholeness from which they came.

# The Longing of Separation

Since the first breath of self-awareness, humanity has lived in the tension between these two lights. Spirit reaching downward to express; matter reaching upward to remember. The human heart became the meeting ground, the altar of their longing. This longing is the ache behind every prayer, every poem, every act of creation. It is not weakness; it is the divine nostalgia of the separated seeking reunion. All seeking whether through love, knowledge, or silence is the movement of one light yearning for the other. When I first felt this longing, I mistook it for emptiness. But emptiness is not absence; it is invitation. It is the space in which the two lights recognize themselves again.

## The Chamber of Union

Deep within the soul lies a chamber that no hand can build. It is formed of silence and guarded by understanding. Here, the seer and the feeler meet. The mind descends in humility; the heart rises in devotion. Their meeting is not of words but of vibration, a quiet merging where thought and feeling become one continuous awareness. The sun pours its fire into the moon, and the moon cools it into form. Will becomes wisdom; emotion becomes clarity. What was once divided now circulates as a single current, rising and descending in perfect rhythm. In this union, light no longer travels it dwells.

## The Dissolving of the Self

When the two lights meet, the mirror shatters. No reflection remains to separate the observer from the observed. There is no "above" and "below," no "inner" and "outer." Only one presence luminous, aware, and whole. The mind, accustomed to division, cannot comprehend it. It feels like a death; the end of all definitions. But what dies is not the self; it is the illusion of separation. The voice that once sought guidance becomes the guidance itself. The question that once echoed in silence becomes the silence that answers. The seeker disappears into what was always seeking.

*"I did not ascend; I dissolved. I did not become light; I remembered I was never anything else."*

# The Birth of the Living Flame

Out of the union of the two lights is born a third a flame that moves without burning, shines without shadow, loves without object. It is the perfected expression of the inner work: consciousness wedded to being, wisdom clothed in compassion. This flame does not belong to the individual. It belongs to life itself. It speaks through the eyes, the hands, the breath through every simple act performed in awareness. The world around begins to reflect its glow. People feel peace in its presence without knowing why. Words become healing without intent. Actions carry power without effort. This is the fruit of the silent work not to withdraw from the world, but to illuminate it quietly from within.

# The Law of Harmony

The one who has united the two lights no longer struggles with opposites. They see that everything serves the same law: that ascent and descent, giving and receiving, silence and speech are all movements of the same eternal breath.

They no longer seek escape from the world, for they have found the world within themselves. Each moment becomes a sacrament of consciousness each breath, a ceremony of union renewed. When the sun and moon share one sky, night and day lose their meaning. Only light remains... complete, eternal, and whole.

## The Unveiling of the Work

In truth, this is what the whole journey has been about. The silent work was never about escape, achievement, or mystical power. It was about remembering the law of harmony written into every cell of being the divine process that turns chaos into clarity, division into unity, darkness into the radiance of understanding. This is the inner science behind every sacred tradition not taught by word, but awakened by experience. It is the art of refining the human into the vessel of the divine, of turning emotion into understanding, desire into direction, and existence into expression. It is not teaching it is a transformation. And its temple is the heart.

# The Eternal Silence

When the marriage is complete, a new silence arises not the silence of absence, but of presence fulfilled. It is the stillness of perfect rhythm, where nothing is sought because all has found its place. The sun and moon rest within one another. The fire and the water sing in harmony. The gardener and the garden have become the same. In that moment, the soul hears the oldest whisper of all:

*"You are the light that balances itself.
You are the work and the worker.
You are the union that makes creation possible."*

And in that knowing, the silent work continues not as effort, but as radiance. Not as discipline, but as being. For once the two lights become one, life itself becomes the sacred flame.

# The Silent Work

# Chapter VIII
# The Union Within: Living Wholeness

All the symbols of light, fire, reflection, and transformation spoken before are ways of describing one thing: wholeness. The silent work is the journey of becoming whole, not by adding anything new, but by healing what has been divided inside us.

In the previous chapter, two lights became one. Now we see what that union really means. It is not a mystical event separate from life. It is life seen clearly, lived consciously, and loved completely.

# The Two Sides of the Self

Every person lives with two sides: the part that acts and the part that feels. The part that plans, builds, and decides, and the part that senses, dreams, and responds. When these two sides are out of balance, life feels divided. We may think clearly but feel disconnected, or feel deeply but lose direction. One part strives, the other resists. The outer world reflects this inner tension as conflict, fatigue, or longing. The purpose of the work is not to suppress one side, but to bring both into cooperation. When thought and feeling move together, will and love become one current. You begin to live from the center instead of the extremes.

# The Meaning of Inner Union

The union within is not about perfection; it's about integration. It means the higher part of you, the conscious, aware presence, has learned to guide the emotional and instinctive parts of you with wisdom and compassion. Your mind begins to serve your heart instead of argue with it. Your emotions begin to support your clarity instead of cloud it. This is the balance of strength and gentleness, reason and empathy, power and peace. When this balance is found, you no longer need to force life. Your actions arise naturally from understanding. The struggle between "who I am" and "who I should be" fades, because both are seen as expressions of the same life unfolding through you.

## The Process of Transformation

Transformation does not happen by sudden miracle. It unfolds quietly, like dawn revealing the world that was already there. Each realization, each honest look at yourself, each moment of awareness brings the divided parts of you closer together. At first, this process can feel like tension. Old patterns resist change. You may feel pulled between the comfort of habit and the call of truth. But this tension is not failure, it is friction turning energy into light. Every time you choose awareness over reaction, compassion over pride, honesty over pretense, you are bringing the two lights within you closer to union. The work is not to fix yourself, but to remember yourself to let the higher and lower parts of your being remember they are one.

## The Heart as the Center of the Work

The mind can think of unity, but only the heart can live it. That is why all transformation returns to the heart. The heart is not just emotion; it is the place of direct knowing. It sees life without analysis, judges without harshness, and forgives without effort. When the heart leads, everything else aligns naturally. To live from the heart is to bring consciousness into every breath, every glance, every word. It does not mean abandoning reason; it means letting reason be guided by love. It means moving through the world not to control it, but to cooperate with it. When the heart opens fully, the walls between inner and outer dissolve. You realize that what you feel within and what you experience without are part of the same current flowing through existence.

# Recognizing Wholeness in Daily Life

Inner union is not a mystical vision, it is lived through ordinary moments.

You recognize it when:

1. You can listen without needing to be right.

2. You can feel pain without turning it into bitterness.

3. You can enjoy success without attachment or pride.

4. You can love without trying to possess.

5. You can act without seeking reward.

In these moments, you are not being "spiritual", you are being whole.

The divine and the human move together as one being.

This is what the work has always aimed toward:

*"Living Naturally in Truth."*

# The End of the Inner War

When awareness and emotion unite, the old inner conflict ends. You no longer fight yourself in secret. There is peace even amid challenge, because you understand that everything serves growth. Failure becomes feedback, not shame. Sadness becomes cleansing, not punishment. Joy becomes gratitude, not possession. You begin to live from the understanding that nothing is against you, everything is working to make you conscious. The very forces that once seemed to oppose you were only parts of yourself asking to be seen. The moment you stop resisting what life reveals, transformation accelerates. You stop searching for peace because peace begins to live through you.

# Living as a Whole Being

To live as a whole being means to walk in both worlds at once. You think, feel, and act as one continuous movement of awareness. You no longer see a line between the sacred and the ordinary; everything becomes sacred. Work becomes service. Relationships become reflection. Challenges become instruction. Even silence becomes full of meaning. This is not an escape from human life; it is the fulfillment of it. The divine expresses itself not by leaving the world, but by living in it consciously through you. You become the bridge between heaven and earth not symbolically, but literally, through the way you move, speak, and love.

# The Real Meaning of "The Work"

All along, the work has been misunderstood as striving or achievement. But the silent work is not effort, it is alignment. It is the daily art of bringing yourself back into harmony with what is true. When you slip into worry, return to presence. When you fall into anger, return to understanding. When you forget who you are, return to stillness. Each return is the work. The work is also the joy of watching yourself evolve from within, of realizing that every part of you, light and shadow alike, was always serving your awakening. This book is not about escaping the human condition, but about revealing the divine intelligence within it. It is about the hidden process that turns ordinary awareness into radiant consciousness. It is the story of the soul remembering itself through experience.

## Living the Union

When the inner marriage is complete, life simplifies. You no longer seek meaning; everything is meaning. You no longer try to shine, you simply stop covering your light. You no longer fear change, you understand that transformation is love in motion. This is not the end of the journey, but the beginning of conscious living. You will still face challenges, but they will no longer divide you. You will still feel emotions, but they will no longer confuse you. You will still live in the world, but now the world will live in you. This is the quiet triumph of the work not to reach heaven, but to reveal it wherever you stand.

*"When the two became one, I became whole.*
*And when I became whole,*
*life itself revealed its oneness."*

# Closing Reflection

The union within is not something to chase; it is what you already are beneath misunderstanding. It is discovered each time you meet life with awareness instead of fear, with openness instead of control. This is what the silent work means the unseen transformation happening every time consciousness replaces reaction, every time understanding replaces judgment, every time peace is chosen over resistance. You are not becoming something new; you are remembering the completeness that was never lost. And as that remembrance deepens, the world around you begins to mirror it for the outer always bends toward the inner light that created it. Wholeness is not an idea to believe; it is a way to live. It is the end of division, the birth of harmony, and the quiet revelation that heaven was never above it was within you, waiting to be seen.

# Gate IV - Where the Two Become One

There comes a moment in this work when the inner journey shifts. Until now, you have learned to listen within, to face your inner mirror, and to live with the light of awareness in daily life. You have tasted silence, clarity, and the first glimpses of inner union. Gate IV is the threshold where these experiences begin to take root as identity. Here, the two lights within you, the one that sees and the one that feels, begin to recognize themselves as one. This Gate is not about becoming something new. It is about remembering what has always been whole within you.

## Seal One - The First Voice Appears

There is a truth you have sensed for a long time, even before you had words for it. You have felt it in quiet moments, in the stillness between thoughts, in the breath that softens your chest, in the peace that arrives when nothing is demanded of you. In those moments, you knew without explanation that something whole was living within you. If you are reading these words now, it is because a part of you is ready to stop seeking wholeness as if it exists somewhere else, and instead begin recognizing it as something already here. You do not need to become anything to be whole. You do not need to fix or purify yourself, or rise above your humanity, to meet the truth of who you are. Wholeness does not arrive through effort. It appears when effort ends. For so long, you believed wholeness would greet you "after". After the healing, after the lessons, after the transformation. But wholeness has never waited at the end of the path. It has walked beside you at every step, quietly asking to be seen. Listen to the voice that speaks to you now, not with urgency, but with familiarity, as if it has spoken within you before: I am the part of you that has always known. The part that does not rush or demand. The part that sees without judging and understands without needing to control. I am not new. You have heard me many times, but mistook me for a moment of clarity, a breath of peace, or a passing insight. Yet I have been here beneath every experience, unchanged. You did not hear me because I do not shout. I do not compete with fear or expectation. I wait for space... like calm after rain, or truth after surrender. Now, you are beginning to hear me as a presence, not a moment.

Pause here.

Not to think, to feel.

I am not speaking to you.

I am speaking from within you.

There is no distance here. No gap to close. What you hear now is your own inner knowing finally given room to speak. Inner wisdom is not earned. It does not appear because you become worthy, disciplined, or awakened. It appears because you become quiet enough to receive what has always belonged to you. You do not need to strain to hear me. I am easiest to hear when you soften. As you read, notice how you are listening. Not with the mind that analyzes, but with the part that remembers. Recognition feels like returning. Wholeness is not something you must reach. It is the nature of your being when you stop dividing yourself. The moment you stop trying to overcome yourself and start listening to yourself instead, the journey changes. You already are what you have been trying to become, not fully lived yet, but fully present. You are not being asked to strive. You are being asked to remember.

## Seal Two - The Soft Recognition of Wholeness

Wholeness rarely arrives with a dramatic breakthrough. It unfolds softly, the way dawn reveals what was always there. You begin to notice subtle changes: A reaction that once felt immediate now pauses before it speaks. A thought that once triggered shame now meets understanding. An emotion that once overwhelmed rises and falls without consuming you. These are not small shifts. They are the first signs that inner alignment is forming. The part of you that feels and the part of you that sees are beginning to acknowledge each other. Before anything can unite, it must first be seen. Take one natural breath, without forcing depth. Notice this simple truth: you can observe your experience without becoming it.

## This awareness is the space where inner union grows.

For years, you believed one part of you needed to win: mind over heart, strength over sensitivity, control over vulnerability. But wholeness is not dominance, it is cooperation.

The mind brings clarity.

The heart brings truth.

One sees the path; the other feels the way.

When they move together, life becomes coherent.

Separation within is the most exhausting weight a human can carry. You are setting that weight down.

Inner union begins the moment you stop trying to fix how you feel and become curious instead. Curiosity opens doors that force keeps shut. Ask gently, "What is this feeling asking from me?" The heart always answers. Sometimes with warmth, sometimes with release, sometimes with clarity that arrives without words. You are not learning something new. You are returning to a way of being you once lived with ease. Before you were taught to split, you lived whole. Wholeness is not a spiritual achievement. It is a return to your natural state.

You are not becoming someone better.

You are becoming someone undivided.

## Seal Three - Living Wholeness in Real Moments

Wholeness becomes real not in silence alone, but in the way you meet your life. It reveals itself through ordinary moments; the same ones that once pulled you out of yourself. Now, those very moments become invitations to remain whole.

### When Wholeness Enters Relationships

You will notice a shift the next time someone speaks to you with emotion, misunderstanding, or frustration. Where the mind once rushed to defend and the heart once rushed to protect, something new appears:

A pause.

In that pause, both your truth and their humanity are held at once.

You listen without abandoning yourself.

You speak without needing to win.

You stay present without shrinking.

Wholeness in relationship looks like:

> "I hear you, and I'm here."

> "I can stay with this feeling without fighting you or myself."

> "We can hold different truths and still remain connected."

You do not lose your voice to maintain peace, nor use your voice to break it.

You respond from clarity, not fear.

Love and truth begin to move together.

## When Emotion Rises Strongly

Wholeness does not remove emotional waves, it

changes your position within them.

Instead of being swept away, you notice the wave rising, cresting, and falling.

Sadness does not collapse you; anger does not own you; fear does not define you.

You feel the emotion fully without turning against yourself for feeling it.

Wholeness in emotion sounds like:

> "This hurts, and I can stay with myself."

> "I can feel this without attacking myself or others."

> "I can let this move through me without becoming it."

Emotion becomes information, not identity.

## When Self-Talk Begins to Shift

The voice inside you changes tone.
What used to be harsh or demanding becomes more like a wise companion.
You do not force positive thinking; the inner narrator simply softens.

Wholeness in self-talk sounds like:

"You're learning. Move gently."

"That was hard. You're still growing."

"You don't need to prove anything right now."

Self-respect becomes natural, not earned.

Inner patience replaces inner punishment.

The mind and heart begin to speak with one voice.

## When the Spiritual Becomes Everyday Life

Wholeness dissolves the line between spiritual moments and ordinary ones.

Meditation does not stay on the cushion.

Stillness follows you into conversations, movement, and choice.

You begin to live with a quiet inner presence, not forced, simply here.

You notice:

A breath before responding

Gratitude between tasks

Awareness while eating, walking, resting

Spirituality becomes less about moments of escape or elevation,

and more about how you move through the world from within.

You do not rise above life , you meet life from your depth.

## The Evidence of Union

You will know wholeness is taking root when:

- You no longer abandon yourself to keep peace

- You no longer need chaos to feel alive

- You can sit with discomfort without losing center

- You choose honesty with yourself over image or approval

None of this comes through force. It comes because something inside you is no longer divided. Wholeness becomes a way of moving, a way of relating, a way of being.

## *Seal Four - Wholeness as Identity*

There comes a moment when the idea of wholeness is no longer something you visit; it becomes the ground you stand on. The shifts are subtle, but unmistakable.

You notice you do not have to "remember" to return to yourself as often. You are already here.

You no longer ask, "What should I be feeling?" You trust what arises.

You no longer seek alignment. You act from alignment.

Wholeness becomes familiar.

It becomes natural.

It becomes you.

### A New Inner Safety

A deep safety emerges not because life grows easier, but because you no longer abandon yourself inside it. Even in uncertainty, there is a quiet steadiness. You may not know the outcome, but you trust that you will remain with yourself. This is the end of self-betrayal. You become a home you can return to.

## The Soft Disappearance of Inner War

Inner conflict fades, not through perfection, but through inclusion. When conflicting thoughts or emotions arise, they no longer tear you apart. You meet them with the same presence that once felt separate. Every part of you is allowed to belong, even before it is fully understood. This is the moment the inner war ends.

## Wholeness Speaks Through You

At this stage, wholeness expresses itself without effort.

People feel calmer around you.

Clarity appears when you speak.

Your presence teaches more than your words.

This is not performance, it is overflow.

Your life becomes the teaching.

The Shift in Who You Believe You Are

You stop identifying as someone "improving" and begin recognizing yourself as someone "remembering."

Improvement strives.

Remembering returns.

Improvement says: "I must change to be enough."

Wholeness says: "I include all of me. And from that love, I grow."

Freedom begins here.

## A Final Truth Before the Practice

You will still forget. You will still drift. But returning will feel natural, like coming home. Not out of discipline, but recognition: Wholeness is my nature. Separation is the illusion I sometimes believe.

# *Gate IV Practice: The Meeting Within*
## *A Guided Inner Experience*

Read slowly. This is not a technique. It is a doorway.

## 1. Entering the Heart

Sit comfortably.

Allow the body to settle without arranging it to be "right."

Let one natural breath move into your chest... not deep, just sincere.

Bring your awareness to the space of your heart, as if you could rest your attention there gently from within.

No need to feel anything special.

Just rest awareness in the heart.

## 2. Becoming Present to Yourself

With your awareness resting in the heart, notice a simple truth:

You are here.

Not seeking.

Not correcting.

Here.

Feel the presence of yourself, meeting yourself. Silently acknowledge:

I am with myself now.

## 3. Softening Into Wholeness

Within the heart, sense the part of you that feels tender, emotional, human.

Acknowledge it with one inner nod.

In this same heart-space, sense the part of you that sees: aware, steady, witnessing.

Acknowledge it too.

Do not merge them.

Do not fix them.

Allow them to stand together in the same space.

Breathe once into this meeting.

## 4. The Inner Union

Silently repeat within:

"I do not need to choose between what I feel and what I know."

Let the words settle.

Allow the feeling part of you and the knowing part of you to sit side by side without forcing union.

If resistance appears, let it be included.

If warmth appears, let it expand.

Wholeness begins with permission, not perfection.

## 5. The Recognition

Shift awareness from the parts to the space that holds both.

Not the feeling.

Not the observer.

But the presence holding them together.

This space is you.

This is wholeness.

Rest here for three slow breaths.

## 6. Sealing the Inner Shift

If you choose, place one palm gently over your heart.

Feel this physical contact as a reminder of the inner truth you touched:

I can stay with myself.

Seal the moment with this inner recognition:

"Wholeness is not something I reach.
It is the one who is here."

## 7. Returning With Wholeness

Become aware of your surroundings again but do not leave the heart to return.

Bring the heart with you.

When your eyes open, open them as if you are still listening from within.

Carry this inner meeting into the next moment, the next breath, the next choice.

# Closing Reflection of Gate IV

You have stepped through an inner threshold. The work ahead will not ask you to become whole, but to live as one who already is. As you move to the next Gate, let this truth accompany you gently:

*"Wholeness is not a state you visit.*
*It is the home you remember."*

# The Silent Work

# Chapter IX
# The Radiance of Being

There comes a dawn after the long night of inner labor. It does not announce itself with thunder or vision. It appears softly, like light touching water as if the whole world had been waiting for your eyes to open. You do not rise into it; it rises through you. For the light you see outside is the same that now lives within.

## The Light That No Longer Seeks

There was once a time when the soul searched for truth.It wandered through teachings, temples, and tears, asking for signs, waiting for revelation. But now, the searching has ended.

The light no longer seeks the sun; it has realized it is sunlight moving through human form. In this stillness, you no longer look for meaning; you become meaning. The outer and inner dissolve into a single clarity: to live is to reveal what you already are.

## The Breath Between Worlds

Every breath now feels like a dialogue between heaven and earth. The inhale gathers from the invisible: wisdom, strength, quiet knowing. The exhale gives it back to creation: kindness, peace, expression. You begin to sense that there is no separation between the breath of man and the breath of the universe. The same rhythm that moves the stars now moves your chest. Each breath becomes prayer without words, a silent exchange between the finite and the infinite. And you understand: you were never alone in the work it was life breathing itself awake through you.

# The World as Reflection

The world does not change because you command it to; it changes because you see it clearly. The anger of others no longer shakes your calm; their light calls to your own. Even sorrow carries beauty now a depth that reminds you how vast compassion truly is. You begin to recognize yourself in everything. The sky is your thought expanded; the earth, your feeling made solid. What once felt outside now speaks your inner language. The world was never separate, it was your reflection, waiting for you to open your eyes with love.

# The Quiet Influence

The one who has found inner peace does not need to speak of it. Their presence becomes its own language. In their silence, others remember something they had forgotten. In their calm, hearts unclench without knowing why. This is how truth moves now. Quietly, invisibly, not through argument but through atmosphere. You realize that to live truthfully is the highest form of teaching. Every gesture, every pause, every gaze carries the pattern of harmony. It is not what you do that transforms the world; it is what you are.

## The Simplicity After the Fire

After the great burning of the self, simplicity returns. The days are ordinary again but now every moment glows from within. You pour water, open a door, greet a stranger and each act feels like prayer, each movement a continuation of the silent work. There is no longer separation between meditation and motion, between the sacred and the daily. The same light shines through both, and because you see it, everything becomes holy. The greatest mastery hides itself in humility, a quiet life lived with extraordinary awareness.

## The Endless Continuation

Illumination is not an ending. It is the beginning of true participation in life. The light within continues to deepen, refining itself through every experience. You will still feel pain, but now pain will polish you instead of breaking you. You will still encounter challenges, but now challenge becomes invitation. The silent work never truly ends it only changes form. From purification to rebirth, from solitude to service, from seeking to being. It becomes the rhythm of your existence breathing, loving, understanding, creating.

## The Light That Walks

When you walk now, the ground feels alive beneath your feet. Each step is answered. Each path reveals itself at the pace of your faith. You do not plan your way; you live it. You no longer ask, "Where am I going?" because you are the way. And wherever the light within you moves, darkness turns transparent, revealing the face of the eternal in all things.

*"Once I sought the light above.*
*Now I see it shining through my own hands."*

# Chapter X
# Living the Radiance

When the light within awakens, life itself becomes the teacher. No longer divided between the sacred and the ordinary, you begin to move through the world as if each step were part of a greater rhythm. The silent work turns outward not as effort, but as expression.

## Presence in the World

To live the radiance is to remain aware while living fully. You speak, work, love, and create, yet beneath every act there is stillness. That stillness is not withdrawal; it is awareness woven into action. You start to notice that peace is portable.

It walks with you into conversation, into challenge, into noise. Even when the outer world trembles, the inner flame remains steady. The true measure of illumination is not visions or words, but how gently you move among others.

## Relationships as Mirrors

People cease to be obstacles or tests; they become mirrors of your own light. When someone angers you, it reveals where your peace still wavers. When someone inspires you, it shows what is awakening within you. Every encounter becomes sacred exchange. Not to judge, but to refine. The awakened being doesn't isolate; they integrate. They bring awareness into the shared spaces of life, turning communication into communion.

## Work as Worship

Whatever you do, healing, teaching, building, parenting, becomes the continuation of your inner work. You no longer labor to survive; you express to serve. Each task becomes a prayer in motion. To live the radiance is to let the divine intelligence move through your ordinary actions. The greater the simplicity, the purer the light that passes through.

## Challenges as Teachers

Illumination doesn't remove difficulty; it transforms its purpose. Challenges still come, but they come as opportunities to strengthen alignment. They remind you to return to center, to breathe, to remember. Suffering once meant punishment; now it becomes purification. Every tension is an invitation to grow more transparent, every conflict a chance to practice presence in motion.

## The Power of Gentle Influence

The radiance you carry influences without intention. It softens spaces, calms storms, heals quietly. Others may feel it without knowing why. This is not personal power, it is harmony made visible. Your task is simply to stay clear enough for that harmony to pass through unhindered.

# Integration as Ongoing Practice

Living the radiance is not a final state; it is a continual alignment. Awareness deepens through humility. The higher the light, the softer the presence. Each day you renew the vow of silence not outer silence, but inner stillness within action. That is how the work remains living: through presence renewed moment by moment.

# Closing Reflection

To live the radiance is to understand that enlightenment is not escape, but engagement life lived consciously. The divine no longer hides behind prayer or meditation; it speaks through your gaze, your touch, your breath.

*"The light I once sought now moves my every motion. The silence I once entered now walks beside me."*

# Gate V - The Return To Presence

You have been searching for something for a long time not with your hands, and not even with your mind, but with a quiet longing you could never fully name. It showed itself in your pauses, in the moments when the world fell silent around you, and for just a breath, you felt something real something untouched.

You have tasted Presence before.
Not in meditation, and not through effort, but in those rare moments when you forgot yourself:

When a sunset held you still.
When a child's laughter opened your heart.

When loss stripped everything unnecessary away.

When silence wrapped around you like clarity.

In those moments, something inside you recognized itself a stillness that did not need identity, a You that did not need a story.

This Gate is not here to teach you Presence.
It is here to help you remember it.

There is a You that existed before thought, before backstory, before becoming.

You have not lost this Self, you only looked away from it.

And now, you are ready to turn toward it again.

## The One Behind Your Thoughts

As you read these words, your mind is processing, interpreting, and understanding. But beneath the movement of the mind, there is a quiet awareness noticing it all aware that reading is happening.

That awareness is not thinking.

It is not judging.

It is simply here.

Notice:

You are aware of your thoughts.

Which means... you cannot be your thoughts.

You are aware of your emotions.

Which means you cannot be your emotions.

You are aware of your body.

Which means you are not limited to the body.

There is a You that sees without effort. A You that has been silently watching your entire life. The same You that was here at age 7, 17, 27 - unchanged, though everything else changed.

That quiet watcher has never aged, never been damaged, never been lost.

It is the one reading these words now.

Let that truth reach you gently.

## A Familiar Presence

If you become still for just a moment  right now, you can feel a subtle aliveness inside you.

Not dramatic. Not mystical. Just a soft hum of being.

It has always been there.

The reason you could never fully abandon yourself...

The reason you survived what should have broken you...

The reason you could still hope after disappointment...

The reason love could still reach you...
is because Presence never left you.

Even when the mind was loud, it whispered.

Even when the heart was tired, it held you.

Even when you forgot, it remembered.

You have been carried by your own Being.

This Gate is not about achieving or earning Presence.

It is about returning to what has always been here.

Stay with this feeling. Do not rush to understand it.

Just breathe once... gently... and notice:

Without effort... You are here.

# When Presence Begins to Reveal Itself

Presence is not something you visit, it is what you are beneath everything you have believed yourself to be.

You were taught to identify with your thoughts, your history, your personality, your roles. You were taught to "be someone." And in trying so hard to become, you drifted away from simply being.

But the one who was aware of all those identities was never lost.

Think of all the different versions of "you" throughout your life:

The child who was curious.

The teenager who was unsure.

The adult who carried responsibility.

Each version had different beliefs, fears, dreams, and preferences.

But something remained the same in all of them; the constant, the silent observer, the awareness that experienced every stage of your life without changing.

That constant presence is the real You.

Not the roles you've played.

Not the image you shaped.

Not the name, the body, or the story.

You could lose all of that today, and still, You would remain.

Feel that.

Not as an idea, but as a quiet recognition.

There is a You that cannot be reduced, that does not come and go, that remains.

## A Glimpse of the Real

You do not have to silence the mind to awaken. You only need to notice that thoughts are not the thinker; they are experiences arising within awareness.

The moment you stop trying to "reach" Presence... Presence reveals itself as what has been here all along.

This realization is subtle like a veil dissolving.

A soft inner exhale.

A sense of "Oh… I'm here."

Right now, pause for only one breath.

Do not change your posture.

Do not change your breathing.

Do not try to "do" anything.

Just notice the simple fact that you exist.

Before thought, before description; you are.

Look from this awareness, not at it.

Even if it's just a glimpse, a brief moment of clarity… something in you felt it.

That is enough.

The Gate has opened.

## When Presence Begins to Live Through You

As Presence grows familiar, subtle changes begin to appear:

You listen differently... not to reply, but to truly hear.

You speak differently... not to prove, but to express truth with clarity.

You move differently, not rushed, but with a natural rhythm that feels aligned.

Life stops feeling like something happening "to" you.

It begins to feel like something happening through you.

Even your thoughts change.

They become fewer, cleaner, quieter. Not because you forced silence, but because the mind relaxes when it is no longer carrying the weight of being "you."

You defend yourself less, because there is less "self" to protect.

You cling less, because nothing needs to be held to be real.

You feel more, but suffer less, because emotions

pass through space instead of through identity. Presence creates space.

And in that space, life becomes kinder.

Not because the world changed but because you stopped fighting with reality.

## The Return to Simplicity

Complexity falls away.

You choose clarity over drama.

Honesty over image.

Stillness over noise.

Not as discipline but as a natural preference.

Moments that once felt ordinary now feel intimate:

The warmth of water on your hands.

The sound of your own footsteps.

The way morning light settles into a room.

This is not "being spiritual."

This is being alive.

Others will feel it.

Some will soften in your presence without knowing why.

Presence needs no announcement.

The river does not declare that it flows.

It simply moves and the world is nourished.

You don't shine to be seen.

You shine because nothing covers the light anymore.

## The Practice: Returning to Presence

This practice is simple.

Not because it is basic but because truth needs no complexity to work.

Read slowly.

1. Sit as you are.
No posture required. No special breathing. Just be here.

2. Let the body be.

Feel its weight. Feel the contact beneath you.
Nothing to change.

3. Notice that you are aware of the body.
The body is being observed. Stay with that
noticing.

4. Now, notice the mind.
Thoughts may move. Images, commentary,
memory, planning.

Do not follow. Just notice: thinking is happening.
You are aware of the thoughts so you are not
inside them.

5. Notice the awareness that notices.
The space in which everything appears.
Do not try to see awareness simply rest as the one
who knows: *"I am aware."*

6. For a moment… drop every description.
Do not define yourself.
Do not refer to past or future.
Do not try to understand.
Just be the awareness that remains.

7. Rest here for a few breaths.
Not as a technique, as yourself.

If the mind returns, notice:
*"I am aware of the mind returning."*

That noticing is already Presence.

A single sentence to remember:
*"I am the one who is aware."*

Recall it, not to think but to remember.

This is the doorway.

Each time you step through it, Presence grows
more familiar.

# *Closing Silence*

Remain here for a moment... without adding anything.

No commentary.

No interpretation.

Just the quiet fact of being.

You are here.

That is enough.

# Chapter XI
# The Silence Beyond Silence

There comes a silence after the silence, not the pause between words, nor the quiet of meditation, but the vast stillness that remains when even light has said its final prayer. Here, the flame no longer flickers. The garden breathes without wind. The soul stands in the center of all things, and realizes it was never separate from them.

## The Vanishing Point

At the edge of illumination, something begins to dissolve. The name you carried, the roles you played, the beautiful story of the seeker all fade like mist before dawn. Nothing is taken; only illusion falls away. The doer disappears, but the work continues.The voice that once whispered truth now becomes the silence that holds it. You are no longer becoming. You are simply being.

## The Ocean Without Shore

In this stillness, there are no boundaries. The self is the horizon, the wave, and the sea at once.

There is no division between awareness and what is seen. Every breath, every sound, every grain of light is part of one unbroken field. Time moves, yet nothing changes. Form shifts, yet essence remains. You discover that eternity was never far away it was hidden in each instant,waiting for the noise of becoming to fade.

*"I entered the silence to find peace,*
*and found there was no one left to seek it."*

## The Return

The radiant one turns inward again, not to retreat, but to rest. Creation breathes out; manifestation then breathes in return. You are both gestures of that eternal breath. Now you understand that the purpose of the journey was never to reach heaven, but to realize that heaven has always been breathing within you. The circle closes not with an ending, but with a quiet smile. The flame returns to the unseen, but its warmth fills everything it touched.

## The Light Beyond Form

Even light must bow before what gave it birth. In the stillness beyond illumination, you feel the presence that cannot be named. The awareness behind awareness, the soundless origin of sound. It does not speak. It does not move.

Yet through it, all things arise and dissolve. This is the truth no teacher can describe, for it can only be remembered when the seeker falls silent enough to hear what never began.

*"There is no path, for I am the way.*
*There is no teacher, for I am the lesson.*
*There is no end, for I am what begins again."*

# The Eternal Rest

In the silence beyond silence, the fire and water are one. The heart and mind are one. The inner and outer no longer exist. There is only the pulse of existence moving through the boundless stillness of being. You rest in that pulse, and it rests in you. The work is done. And yet, it continues forever, quietly, through every soul that remembers the stillness within.

*"The Silence was the First Teacher.*
*The Silence Will Be The Last."*

# Chapter XII
# The Continuation

When the search ends, life goes on. The sun still rises, the body still breathes, the world still asks its daily questions. But something within you has changed completely. You no longer look at life as a puzzle to solve, but as a mystery to participate in. The silence you once entered during meditation never leaves you now it walks with you through every moment.

## Living After the Work

The idea of "the work" begins to fade. You don't think about transformation anymore; you live it. You don't analyze awareness; you rest in it. You find yourself meeting people with more patience, speaking less, listening more, feeling compassion even when others don't understand you. That is how the silent work continues not as effort, but as quiet understanding expressed through simple kindness. Your light doesn't need attention; it just shines.

# Nothing to Prove

You stop needing to convince anyone of what you've learned. Truth doesn't need defense; it reveals itself through presence. You realize that everyone is walking their own path, and your only task is to walk yours in peace. You no longer try to be spiritual; you simply are. You laugh more easily, love more deeply, and move through the world without needing to control it. Freedom feels natural now not as rebellion, but as acceptance.

# The Quiet Flow of Purpose

Purpose no longer feels like a goal it feels like movement. You don't have to find your place in the world; you create it by being fully yourself. The divine will you once seek to align with now moves through your smallest choices. Sometimes that means speaking truth. Sometimes it means silence. Sometimes it means rest. But whatever it is, it comes from peace, not fear. That is how you know you are still walking in light.

## The Gentle Rhythm of Return

You still have emotions, but they don't rule you. You still have thoughts, but they pass like clouds. You still face uncertainty, but it no longer shakes you. You've learned to return to center over and over again to breathe, to observe, to remember. That rhythm is the living silence. The more you practice it, the less it feels like practice. It becomes your way of being.

## Becoming the Silence

There comes a day when you realize that you don't visit silence anymore; you are silence. It's in your words, your laughter, your eyes. It's not something you enter; it's what you carry. And people feel it, even if they can't name it. They feel calm around you, not because you're special, but because you've stopped fighting what is. This is how the silent work continues in the world Through those who live peace instead of talking about it.

## Closing Reflection

The journey ends, but the life of awareness continues. You live, love, and breathe the same as before, but now everything you touch carries the quiet vibration of truth. You understand that transformation was never about leaving the world, but about returning to it with open eyes and an open heart. The silent work goes on in every breath, in every act of kindness, in every moment when someone chooses understanding over fear.

> *"The silence remains.*
> *It listens through us.*
> *And through that listening,*
> *the world remembers itself."*

# Gate VI: Returning to Being Human
## Seal One — Integration

There comes a point on this journey where the most honest next step isn't to "rise" any higher, but to come back down to earth = gently, humbly, and fully as yourself.

After everything you've seen, felt, released, and become, it's easy to quietly form a new identity around it, a "spiritual" one. Not out of arrogance, but out of habit. You've worked so hard to awaken that part of you may fear becoming "ordinary" again, as if the light could be lost.

But here's the truth a friend would tell you, softly and without judgment:

You don't need to hold on to a version of yourself that is "enlightened," "awake," or "beyond."

The moment you try to keep the light, it dims.

The moment you try to be the light, it becomes another role to perform.

The real sign that the work has ripened is not

how elevated you feel but how natural you become.

You laugh again.

You breathe without effort.
You stop trying to be wise and simply become honest.

You stop trying to show peace and instead choose kindness.

The silence you found in stillness is still here but now it wears your normal life comfortably.

You don't need to speak gently to prove inner calm.

You don't need to appear humble to show growth.

You don't need to "stay spiritual" to remain true.

You can just be... a human being who remembers.

This Gate is a soft landing, a reminder that the journey was never meant to carry you away from life, but to guide you back into it with more tenderness, clarity, and simplicity than before.

Not higher.

Not special.

Just real.

If the earlier Gates helped you open, transform, and expand, this one helps you exhale. It brings your feet all the way to the ground, where your heart can rest and your life can breathe again.

## *Seal Two — The Seal*

Let this truth meet you without resistance:

You don't need to stay "awake" to be whole.

You don't need to maintain an identity of wisdom, peace, or light.

You don't need to be seen as evolved, conscious, or transformed.

The work was never meant to turn you into someone extraordinary.

It was meant to return you to the simplicity of being fully yourself without the inner war.
You can release the need to "hold on" to all you've learned.

What is real will remain.

What was effort can fall away.

You don't need to protect your growth.

You don't need to perform your stillness.

You don't need to preserve your light.

You are allowed to be ordinary again.

Not the old ordinary, but the kind that is Still, honest, and quietly free.

Nothing you gained can be lost because you were what you were seeking.

This Gate seals not with elevation, but with a return.

## *Seal of the Gate*

This is a two-part practice: one deep exercise for today, and a simple daily reinforcement.

### Part A: One-Time Deep Practice - "Setting Down the Robe"

Give yourself 10–12 minutes.

1. Sit comfortably, not in a "meditative" pose, just as a regular person sitting to rest.

2. Place your hands on your lap, palms down. Feel your weight supported.

3. Speak gently to yourself (aloud or silently):
"I don't need to be anything right now."

4. Let your face relax. Your jaw. Your shoulders. Your breath.

5. Now recall one way you still try to appear awakened, calm, or conscious.
Don't judge it just recognize it.

6. With your next exhale, imagine setting that identity down beside you, like removing a robe you no longer need to wear.

Sit for a moment in the simple truth of being nobody special... just here.

Let that feel safe.

Let that feel enough.

## Part B: Daily Reinforcement - "The Ordinary Breath" (30–60 seconds)

Once a day, during something completely normal (washing hands, walking to your car, waiting in line):

1. Take one soft breath.

2. Think this quietly:
"I am allowed to be human."

No performance.
No posture.
No special voice.
Just you.

The more you practice this, the more natural life will feel again.

Gate VI closes when you feel the ground beneath you and trust it.

When being human feels like home again, you will know this Gate has opened.

# Chapter XIII
# The Veil and the Two Natures**

This book was not written in a straight line. It moves like breath, inward and outward, veiled and revealed. The first chapter of each pair speaks through symbols to awaken consciousness. The second speaks through clarity to instruct the intellect. Together they mirror the two sides of human nature, the inner and the outer, the silence and the word.

## The Language of Symbols
### Speaking to Consciousness

The veiled chapters cannot be fully understood

through analysis. They are written in the language of symbols, which speaks directly to the soul beneath the noise of thought. Symbols are living forms. They reach beyond intellect to stir memory in the deeper layers of being. They were not written for you to figure out; they were written for you to remember through. When you encounter an image that seems strange, a line that feels deeper than it sounds, pause and feel it. Do not demand meaning. Allow recognition to rise in silence. This is how consciousness learns. It does not study; it recalls. The symbolic chapters communicate through rhythm, tone, and feeling. They are invitations to a dimension of knowing that the mind cannot enter without surrender.

## The Language of Clarity
### Speaking to the Intellect

The unveiled chapters come after the veiled ones for a reason. They help the intellect translate what consciousness has already absorbed. They ground the inner experience in words and comprehension, allowing what was awakened in silence to take form in understanding. These chapters speak directly to your reason, guiding the thinking mind to cooperate with the inner knowing. They ensure that the work does not drift into abstraction. The intellect, when properly guided, becomes the faithful servant of consciousness; giving body to spirit and form to insight.

## Piercing the Veil

To truly benefit from The Silent Work, one must move beyond reading altogether. You must let the book read you. When consciousness and intellect begin to merge, the words become mirrors; you will start to see your own reflection in the text. To pierce the veil means to move past the need for explanation; to enter the space between words where meaning is born.
When you can sit in that stillness without searching, you have entered the real classroom. There, silence teaches in a way that no sentence ever could. Until that time, remain silent unless moved by consciousness to speak. Speech that

arises from intellect alone perpetuates illusion; speech born of silence carries power.

# The Two Natures
## The Ego

The ego is the outer instrument: the identity shaped by experience, attachment, and expectation. It speaks first, reacts quickly, fears loss, and clings to control. It creates separation so that consciousness may have something to awaken from. But when ego rules, life becomes noise; endless motion without meaning. The ego believes it is alive because it moves. Consciousness knows it is alive because it is. Consciousness is the silent watcher behind every experience. It observes the rise and fall of thoughts and emotions without becoming them. It is still, luminous, and eternal. It cannot be threatened, praised, or broken. When a person begins to live from consciousness, the ego is not destroyed; it is refined. The self becomes transparent enough for the light to shine through it. In this harmony, the human and divine meet.

# The Purpose of the Structure

The alternating rhythm of this book, one chapter veiled, one unveiled, is not literary; it is alchemical. It trains both of your natures simultaneously: The veiled chapters awaken consciousness through symbols. The unveiled chapters train intellect through reason. By the end, if you have read with both heart and mind, something new will awaken: a listener between the two. A self that no longer asks "What does this mean?", but rather feels, "I have always known this." That is the goal of the silent work.

# The Role of the Gates

Following each veiled and unveiled chapter, the Gates are placed to ensure the teachings become lived experience rather than concepts. The two chapters act as keys. One awakening inner awareness and the other clarifying understanding. And the Gate that follows shows you how to embody what was revealed. Without the Gates, the reader might understand the ideas but never become them. The Gates exist to transition the teachings from knowledge into practice, guiding you to integrate the silent and spoken lessons into everyday life.

## The Language of Symbols

The symbols within The Silent Work are not decorations. They are mirrors of invisible processes happening inside the reader. Each symbol speaks in two directions at once: to the intellect, it is metaphor; to the soul which is consciousness itself it is direct communication. These images are written in the oldest language there is the language of the inner world. They are not meant to be decoded or explained too soon. Instead, they are to be experienced, for they reflect the movement of your own awareness as it purifies, expands, and remembers itself. Below are the primary symbols used throughout this work. They are not lessons to learn, but keys that open inwardly the moment you recognize their meaning in yourself.

# The Flame

The flame is conscious awareness the soul awakened within matter. It represents the living light that perceives, understands, and transforms. When it is small, it flickers in reaction to outer winds; when it grows, it becomes steady, independent, and luminous. To tend the flame is to keep your awareness clear. To guard the light of knowing from being dimmed by distraction.

# The Water

Water represents the subconscious, the emotional depth of the soul. It is receptive, reflective, and alive. When still, it mirrors the flame perfectly; when agitated, it distorts its reflection. In the silent work, one learns not to suppress the waters but to calm them allowing the subconscious to become transparent to the light of consciousness.

# The Fire

Fire is purification. The force that burns away falsehood and releases truth. It is pain turned into wisdom, desire transformed into will. Fire tests what is real; only what is true can endure its heat. Through fire, the soul sheds illusion until only essence remains.

# The Garden

The garden symbolizes the inner field of cultivation, the place within where transformation grows. Every thought is a seed, every emotion a root, every intention a gardener's touch. Neglect brings confusion; care brings beauty. The garden thrives when consciousness tends to it daily with attention and love.

# The Mirror

The mirror is self-observation. It shows the image of the ego without judgment, revealing what has been projected outward. To gaze into the mirror is to meet yourself with honesty, not to condemn what you see, but to understand it. When the gaze is steady, reflection becomes revelation.

# The Two Lights

The two lights, golden and silver, represent the mind and the heart, or the active and receptive aspects of being. The golden light is intellect, focus, and expression. The silver light is intuition, reflection, and feeling. When the two are united, they form the full radiance of balanced awareness. The soul acting as one harmonious force.

# The Silence

Silence is the resting state of consciousness. It is the ground beneath every thought and the space from which every word arises. In silence, the soul remembers itself as presence. Here, knowing is immediate; understanding has no need for language. All true transformation begins and ends in silence.

# The Circle

The circle represents continuity and completion. It has no start or end, symbolizing the eternal rhythm of creation: inhalation and exhalation, birth and return. The circle is life as Spirit's breath; the endless pulse of expansion and contraction through which the universe lives. To see life as circular is to understand that nothing is lost, only transformed.

# The Light and the Shadow

Light and shadow are two movements of one consciousness. Light reveals; shadow conceals. But both are necessary for vision. The shadow teaches humility and depth; the light teaches clarity and revelation. When the two are reconciled, wisdom is born and perception becomes whole.

# The Soul (Consciousness)

The soul is the conscious awareness itself: the experiencer, the knower, the perceiver. It is not a thing that can be located; it is the living field in which all things appear. The soul feels, learns, and remembers its own divine origin through experience. It is both the student and the classroom. The part of you that transforms through every lesson of life. When the soul is awake, it recognizes that every event, thought, and emotion was only consciousness teaching itself to see.

## The Spirit (Breath)

Spirit is the breath of life. The movement of consciousness through existence. It is invisible, yet it animates everything. Every inhale draws Spirit inward; every exhale releases it back to the whole. Spirit is the pulse of creation. The constant reminder that awareness is alive. When one becomes conscious of the breath, Spirit and Soul unite, and life itself becomes meditation.

# The Silence Between Symbols

Beyond all of these is the final symbol; the space between them. This silence is where meaning lives before it becomes a word, and where word returns when meaning is complete. It is the original breath before the first sound and after the last. When you rest in that silence, you are no longer reading The Silent Work. You are living it.

*"The symbols were never lessons.
They were reflections of what you already are -
Soul, the awareness that sees;
Spirit, the breath that moves;
Silence, the truth that remains."*

# Author's Reflection
# How the Work Found Me

I know you may be wondering what brought me to these so-called esoteric sciences. The truth is, it began not with ancient symbols or hidden orders, but with my own study of psychology. Freud and Jung both practiced a method known as psychoanalysis. The exploration of the subconscious through the patient's own thoughts and memories. I found something profoundly spiritual in that idea. It was not just science; it was self-discovery. Where others saw the mind, I saw the soul. So I became my own patient. I called it self-psychoanalysis. My approach was not through notebooks or dialogue but through meditation the art of listening inward.

At a certain point in my life, I began to feel deeply triggered. Emotions that had slept beneath the surface for years started to rise old memories, unhealed pain, anger, guilt, grief. They came in waves, and I didn't know what to do with them. When I tried to speak about these experiences with those close to me, I was dismissed. I heard phrases like, "Everyone has problems," or "You're overthinking it." So I turned inward not out of pride, but necessity. Through meditation, I began traveling deep into my subconscious mind, using the method described in **Chapter V**: **The Hidden Garden**. That chapter became real for me long before it was written. I would enter silence, allow the mind to still, and then let one memory rise, usually one charged with emotion. Once it appeared, I didn't resist it. I didn't analyze or escape it. Instead, I allowed myself to feel everything I had once been too afraid to feel. Then, using the superconscious the higher awareness within us I would revisit that day, that scene, that moment in time. I watched it unfold again, but this time, I remained fully present. I felt every sensation I had once buried, and I stayed with it until the energy behind it dissolved. What began as pain would eventually turn to stillness what I came to call peace. I repeated this process again and again with different memories, emotions, and fragments of the past. Slowly, something miraculous began to happen: the heavy feelings that once ruled my life started to lose their power. The noise within became silence. The silence became clarity. And in that clarity, I realized something that changed me forever: psychology is the study of the soul. Not merely the study of behavior, but the observation of consciousness itself. Behavior is only the surface; beneath it lies the entire universe of human experience. That understanding led me beyond textbooks and theories. It led me into the deeper layers of human nature, the realm that ancient mystics and philosophers had always spoken of. I began to see that what modern psychology calls the subconscious, earlier traditions called the soul's shadow, and what we call the superconscious, they called the divine spark or higher self. From that moment, my study of psychology and my inner work became one and the same. The sciences of the mind and the sciences of spirit were never meant to be divided; they are two languages describing the same mystery. Through these realizations, I stumbled upon what the ancients symbolized as the art of turning lead into gold. The lead was not metal, it was the weight of my own unresolved self. The gold was the light that appeared when that weight was transformed into understanding. That process, slow, internal, invisible became what I call The Silent Work. This book is the story of that process. It is not a doctrine or belief system; it is a reflection of what happens when one turns inward and begins to refine the raw material of the human soul into clarity and peace. If, while reading these pages, something stirred within you, confusion, resistance, curiosity, even emotion, that is the beginning of your own silent work. Do not turn away from it. Continue to seek whatever it is you feel rising within. Follow it honestly. It will take you exactly where you need to go. If, however, this book left you untouched, that's alright too. Not every seed is meant to bloom in every season. Whether you agree, disagree, understand, or question, it makes no difference. What matters is that you listened long enough to touch silence even for a moment. Because in the end, that is where all journeys lead. Silence is where the work begins. And silence is where it ends. I began with silence. I ended with silence. Everything in between was only remembering what it meant to be whole.

## The Fire That Grows in Silence

I will reveal one mystery not yet known to man, though it has been spoken of in scripture, hidden in parable, and veiled in ancient symbols for the wise to uncover. The burning fire often written of is not a flame of destruction, but the fire of the soul itself. The living light of consciousness within man. This fire purifies, transforms, and gives life to awareness. Yet it is the silence that feeds it. When one begins to speak of the inner transformation, the fire diminishes. Words disturb its rising, as if the wind that sustained it suddenly ceases to blow. But when one remains silent, the flame strengthens in stillness, unseen yet more radiant than before. This is the sacred law of the soul: speech disperses power; silence gathers it. Only the ego needs to prove, to explain, to be heard.

Consciousness simply is.

It burns in quiet certainty, saying nothing but I Am. Thus the silent one becomes a living altar. The fire within ascending toward the unseen Source. This is the mystery once hidden, now revealed.

*"The Rest is for the Reader to find."*

# About Knowledge King

Knowledge King holds a bachelor's degree in psychology and is currently pursuing a graduate degree in Clinical Mental Health Counseling. He is a Registered Behavior Technician (RBT) who works closely with autistic children, supporting development through evidence-based, behaviorally informed practice. His professional background is rooted in disciplined observation, psychological structure, and respect for the inner world of the individual.

Alongside his clinical training, Knowledge has maintained a lifelong interest in depth psychology and the inner processes of transformation. This led him to the work of Carl Jung, whose writings on the psyche, symbolism, and the hidden dimensions of human experience deeply influenced his understanding of psychological development. Jung's exploration of myth, symbol, and the unseen layers of consciousness provided a framework through which inner transformation could be approached without superstition or spectacle.

The Silent Work emerges at the intersection of psychological discipline and inner practice. It does not seek to instruct, persuade, or initiate, but to recognize states of being that arise through sustained inner labor. The work is written for those who sense that transformation occurs quietly, beyond performance and proclamation, and that the most profound changes take place where words grow sparse.